Contents

CONTENTS

A GUIDE TO THE BENEFITS OF

CHARITABLE STATUS

by
Michael Norton

Directory of Social Change

A GUIDE TO THE BENEFITS OF CHARITABLE STATUS

Written and designed by Michael Norton

Cover design by Ruth Lowe

First published 1983

The Directory of Social Change is a registered educational charity.

The Directory of Social Change, 9 Mansfield Place, London NW3 1HS

ISBN 0 907164 09 9

Photoset by Scarborough Typesetting Services, Scarborough, North Yorkshire

Printed and bound in Great Britain by Biddles of Guildford

British Library CIP Data
Norton, Michael
A guide to the benefits of charitable status.
1. Charitable uses, trusts and foundations
I. Title
344.106'64   KD1487
ISBN 0–907164–09–9

The figures given in this book for tax rates and thresholds relate to 1982–83.

The author acknowledges the assistance of the Inland Revenue, the Charity Commission, H.M. Customs and Excise, the Department of Health and Social Security and the Department of the Environment in reading and commenting on parts of the manuscript of this book.

CONTENTS

Introduction

Many organisations rush to get charitable status simply because they feel that in some way it is appropriate for them. They may understand some of the restrictions that it places on what they do, but often they are sadly unaware of the range of benefits and the opportunities that their charitable status offers them. Similarly, long-established organisations which are hard pressed for funds should examine whether they are obtaining the full range of reliefs that are available and whether they are making use of the opportunities for fund-raising that exist as a result of their charitable status.

This book seeks to explain the more important advantages of charitable status and to show when they apply and how charities might organise themselves to exploit them to the full. The benefits fall into three distinct categories:

1. Saving money

There are several important benefits which enable a charity to save money on its expenditure. This is the first area that should be looked at as it is usually easier for an organisation to save money than to raise money; and once a charity has organised itself to take advantage of these benefits, it will be able to enjoy the fruits of this work over the years. The most important of these reliefs are:

Rate relief;

Relief from National Insurance Surcharge;

Relief from tax on investment income and bank interest;

Relief from tax on the profits of trading (if the trading activity is organised in such a way as makes this possible);

Certain VAT reliefs.

2. Reliefs to donors

Certain reliefs are available to donors to encourage them to give. These were greatly extended in the *1980 Finance Act* as a means of encouraging charitable activity without the government making more money available to charities in the form of direct grants. These reliefs work in two ways. They are a form of matching funds where the government provides tax relief to enhance the value of what the charity itself can raise; and they also encourage donors to give on the basis that certain types of donation are tax free, whereas otherwise the donor might be liable to a high rate of tax in respect of the amount of income or capital donated. These reliefs are available for:

Deeds of Covenant;

Lifetime capital gifts;

Legacies and bequests on death;

Interest-free loans.

3. Opportunities for fund-raising

There are many important opportunities for raising money that are extended to charities, and in some instances to other forms of good cause organisations. Not all are appropriate to every charity, but many charities could make use of more of these ways of raising money than they currently do. The most important of these opportunities are:

Grants and donations from tax-exempt sources such as grant-making trusts and from other grant-making organisations whose policy it is to give to charities;

Collecting from the public via street collections and house-to-house collections;

Raffles and lotteries;

Other forms of gaming and competitions.

Some of these benefits are obviously more important than others.

INTRODUCTION

Which benefits offer the best opportunities to any charity will depend on how it raises its money and how it spends it. Overall though the major benefits, aside from the ability to get grants, are:

(a) **Income Tax and Capital Gains Tax relief** on investment and rental income and bank interest. The Charities Aid Foundation give a figure of £765 million for the gross value of this income for 1980–81. With the basic rate of Income Tax and Capital Gains Tax both at 30 per cent, the value of this relief must be very considerable.

(b) **Capital Transfer Tax relief** on legacies and lifetime gifts of capital. The legacy income of charities is estimated at £260 million annually, and the relief must be worth around £50 million plus annually.

(c) **Income Tax relief** including Higher Rate tax relief on covenants. The figure for covenants is around £150 million annually and will expand as more people take advantage of Higher Rate Relief and the reduction of the minimum period to four years. This relief must be worth between £40 million and £50 million annually.

(d) **Rate relief** on premises occupied by charities and used for charitable purposes. The total value of rate relief enjoyed by charities annually is in the region of £80 million.

(e) **Relief from Employer's National Insurance Surcharge.** This would amount to between £10 million and £20 million annually if one-third of the estimated expenditure of £2.6 billion spent by charities covers salaries.

Some of the available benefits are clearly defined and easy to obtain. Others involve an interplay of factors, and even conflicting definitions as to what is tax exempt as defined by the two main taxation authorities (the Inland Revenue in respect of Income Tax, etc. and Customs and Excise in respect of VAT). This book tries to guide the reader through what is an exceedingly complex technical field and at the same time offer some practical advice on how to take best advantage of the situation. In certain circumstances there are 'grey areas' where the situation is unclear, and the advantages that can be gained by charities are greater than what might be available under any strict interpretation of the law. In particular the paying of subscriptions under Deed of Covenant and the treatment of sponsorship as either a proper business expense or a pure donation are examples of this, and it would probably be to the disadvantage of charities to seek any clarification in these situations.

There are certain underlying issues which are obviously of importance in connection with charitable status. Should an organisation be set up as a charity or should it operate outside the charitable net? This is a decision which each and every organisation has to make for itself. The decision will be based on the balance of advantages and disadvantages of charitable status, the financial benefits that will accrue to it on the one hand, and the constraints on undertaking certain activities it might wish to undertake on the other. And if it does decide to register, the charity would do well to review periodically the advantages it is obtaining from its charitable status and whether it is able to undertake all the activities it wishes to do.

If an organisation is not a charity, it can do what it wants so long as it is legal; but it cannot enjoy the benefits of charitable status. The Joseph Rowntree Social Service Trust is a good example of this. The Trust pays tax on its income, but supports centre party politics in this country, freedom movements abroad and all sorts of campaigning projects which would not be allowed if it were a charity. This book does not discuss the decision to register, but it examines the benefits that are available once an organisation has decided to operate as a charity.

Equally the need for charity law reform is not discussed. Charities today have to operate within a legal framework which was originally drawn up in 1601. Although the concept of charity has evolved over the years, there is a view that what is held to be charitable by the Charity Commission and the Courts is not wholly in line with what some people see as the present-day needs of society. In addition to the issue of charity law reform, many charities also see a need for tax reform; and of particular note are the campaigns to reform VAT, which are currently being run by arts organisations (with regard to VAT on ticket sales at performances) and by an ad hoc 'VAT Reform Group' (for tax relief on the VAT costs of providing charitable services).

This book takes the tax advantages as they exist. It does not discuss whether they are satisfactory or whether charities should be given further concessions. But it does argue that there is plenty of scope for charities to use the concessions that do exist to better advantage. And in Appendix 2 which discusses political activities by charities, we also show that the possibilities exist for charities to organise themselves in such a way that any non-charitable activity they wish to undertake is separated out, such that they do not jeopardise their charitable status and are still able to obtain the benefits of charitable status in respect of their charitable work.

Michael Norton
October 1982

1. Rates

Under *Section 40* of the *1967 General Rate Act* charities are given rate relief on premises occupied by them which are used wholly or mainly for charitable purposes. Two forms of rate relief are available:

Mandatory relief of **50 per cent** of the rates chargeable, which a charity is **entitled to as of right** provided notice in writing is given to the rating authority; and

Discretionary relief of **up to 50 per cent** of the rates chargeable, which is available **at the sole discretion of the local rating authority**.

In addition to the general provisions for rate relief there are certain provisions for granting relief from rates to charity shops which sell mainly donated goods. These provisions for rate relief apply only to the local authority rates. They do not apply to the water and sewage charge which is administered and charged for separately by local water authorities, and where no reliefs are available to charities.

The two-fold system of mandatory and discretionary relief stems from the history of rate concessions granted to charities. Earlier this century although local authorities were unable to grant rate relief to charities, they were able to give a sympathetic low valuation to premises occupied by charities. This did not provide for full rate relief, but many charities were able to obtain a substantial benefit from the low valuation of their premises. There were two problems: firstly valuation practice varied widely between local authority and local authority; and secondly there was no legal entitlement for charities to receive any rate relief at all. In 1948 responsibility for valuing land and property was transferred to the Inland Revenue. The intention was to provide a centralised valuation of property for rating purposes, based on a uniform method of assessment through-out the country. Sympathetic undervaluation of charity property was then no longer possible, and a temporary system of rebate dependent on the degree of undervaluation they had previously enjoyed was introduced, so that charities which had been receiving sympathetic treatment from their local authorities should not lose out. At the same time a more permanent solution was sought.

The present system was first introduced in the *1961 Rating and Valuation Act*. For the first time it granted charities a statutory entitlement to rate relief. It incorporated both a national and a local element for the relief granted to charities. Nationally it gave charities a 50 per cent relief dependent only on their charitable status, in order to give charities as a group some benefit as a matter of national policy. At a local level it gave local authorities the power to determine for themselves whether to allow any additional benefit to charities situated within their area.

The cost of mandatory relief (the national element) is met by central government. Local authorities do not receive a direct pay-ment in respect of the mandatory rate relief they have given to charities in their area. The mechanism by which they are compen-sated is that where the authority is in receipt of Rate Support Grant resources element, the calculation of the block grant that is payable takes special account of the mandatory rate relief that has been granted in the local authority area. The cost of discretionary rate relief (the local element) is borne by the local rating authority, and is written off as a loss on collection in calculating the penny rate.

The total Rateable Value allowed for mandatory rate relief in 1980–81 was £41.6 million. This is 50 per cent of the Rateable Value of the buildings on which relief was given, and the benefit to the charities was the Rateable Value multiplied by the rate poundage in the rating district concerned. If the average rate poundage were £1.20, this would give a total value of mandatory relief of around £50 million annually. No figures are available for the value of dis-cretionary relief to charities.

The situation on rate relief for charities appears clear-cut. And indeed for most charities for most of the property they occupy they will be able to obtain partial or full rate relief. In fact the situation is far more complex than can be set down in a single paragraph. There are instances where rate relief is available to non-charitable organis-ations. There are instances where the premises occupied by the charity is not deemed to be used wholly or mainly for charitable purposes, and as a consequence rate relief is not available. And there is the possibility that, where full rate relief cannot be obtained, in certain circumstances an organisation might be able to obtain a full rate rebate under different legislation altogether. In this section we examine in detail the ramifications of rates in relation to property occupied by charities and other benevolent organisations.

Mandatory rate relief

For all charities there is an absolute entitlement to rate relief under *Section 40(1)* of the *1967 General Rate Act*. This mandatory rate relief is for 50 per cent of the local authority rate payable on premises occupied by the charity **where the premises are being occupied wholly or substantially for charitable purposes**. The charity may also be able to obtain further relief from the remaining 50 per cent of its rates bill from its local authority under their powers to grant discretionary rate relief. In Northern Ireland the level of mandatory relief is 100 per cent, so where a charity is eligible for relief, no rates are payable at all.

The charity has to claim mandatory rate relief from its local rating authority (the District or Borough Council area within which the premises are situated). The charity can only make a claim for the rate period in which the claim is being made and for any subsequent periods. (The rate year runs from the 1st April to the following 31st March.) It cannot claim rate relief retrospectively, for previous rate periods where it failed to make a claim or where it was unable to make a claim because it had not yet been given charitable status.

The uses of the premises for which rate relief is and is not available is discussed subsequently. First we will examine in detail the organisations for which this mandatory rate relief is available:

1. Registered charities

If an organisation has obtained registration as a charity with the Charity Commission, this is deemed to be conclusive evidence of its charitable status. And it will then be automatically entitled on application to the rating authority to the 50 per cent mandatory rate relief on premises occupied by it and used by it wholly or substantially for charitable purposes.

2. Charities not obliged to register

Certain charitable organisations are not obliged to register with the Charity Commission. These include:

(a) *All charitable organisations in Scotland and Northern Ireland:* No registration procedures yet exist for charities situated in these parts of the United Kingdom. The jurisdiction of the Charity Commission extends only to England and Wales.

(b) *Certain excluded and excused charities in England and Wales:* There are a number of **'excluded charities'** which do not fall within the definition of a charity under the 1960 Charities Act which are therefore unable to register as charities. There are also certain classes of charities which are 'excused' from registration, and these fall into four categories:

  (i) Exempt charities;

  (ii) Excepted charities;

  (iii) Small charities;

  (iv) Places of Religious worship

  (See Appendix 1 for details of where a charity is excluded from or excused registration).

A charitable organisation in England and Wales in any one of the four excused categories may apply to the Charity Commission for voluntary registration as a means of proving its charitable status. Where the charity does not wish to or cannot register voluntarily, the charitable status will have to be determined by the Inland Revenue for tax purposes and by the local rating authority for rating purposes.

The organisation may already have obtained a determination from the Inland Revenue as to its charitable status — for example, if it has made a claim for a tax refund on a covenant payment or in respect of its investment income which has been accepted by the

Inland Revenue, or if it has approached the Inland Revenue for a decision to determine whether or not it is liable to pay, say, Capital Gains Tax. Where the Inland Revenue has decided that the organisation is charitable, this fact should obviously be put to the local rating authority when the charity is applying for mandatory rate relief. Where the organisation has obtained no prior determination as to its charitable status from another source, the local rating authority will then have to determine for itself whether the organisation is charitable, and as a consequence whether it is entitled to mandatory rate relief.

The most usual form of unregistered charity is the small charity excused registration. It should be noted that one of the conditions of non-registration of a small charity is that it is not in occupation of land or property − and if this is the case, the charity will not be paying rates. But there are other charities which do not have to register which find themselves having to get the local rating authority to determine their charitable status, and as a consequence to decide whether they are entitled to mandatory rate relief. Probably the most common instance where this happens is for charitable housing associations registered under the *Industrial and Provident Societies Act*.

The *1967 General Rate Act* specifically states that mandatory rate relief shall be granted to organisations established for charitable purposes only, and this will be the central argument in deciding whether the organisation is entitled to mandatory rate relief. The Charity Commission and the Inland Revenue will only grant charitable status to organisations which have been established for charitable purposes only. Where the organisation is seeking a determination of its charitable status from its local rating authority, it is not sufficient that the occupation of the premises is for charitable purposes only, but in addition the organisation itself must be constitutionally unable to undertake any non-charitable activity. So the argument that the premises are being used for charitable purposes on its own will fail.

3. Charitable organisations that have failed to obtain registration.

As we have seen, when an organisation obtains registration as a charity this is deemed to be conclusive evidence of its charitable status. If, however, the organisation fails to obtain registration with the Charity Commission for whatever reason, this is not deemed to be conclusive evidence that the organisation is not a charity.

During the registration process, the Inland Revenue will have been consulted about the application for charitable status, and it is unlikely to take a different view from the Charity Commission once the decision on registration has been made. But there is nothing to stop the organisation approaching its local rating authority for mandatory rate relief on the basis that it believes that it is a charity, even when it has failed to obtain registration as a charity with the Charity Commission. The local rating authority will then have to determine for itself whether it also believes the organisation to be a charity, and is therefore entitled to mandatory relief. In this circumstance the most likely course of action for the local rating authority is to ask the organisation for its charity number; and when the organisation is unable to provide this, the local authority will then in all probability decide that there is no entitlement to mandatory relief.

But that need not be the end of the matter. The organisation can then take the matter to court for decision. There is a precedent for this course of action in the 1974 case of *Over Seventies Housing Association v Westminster City Council* where the housing association having failed to get registration as a charity asked the court for a determination on the matter for rating purposes. It must be said that an organisation taking this course of action is not very likely to succeed.

In a similar vein, for a charity which is having difficulty in obtaining charitable status and where negotiations with the Inland Revenue and the Charity Commission are taking years rather than weeks, the organisation can still put in a claim for rate relief from the local rating authority. Again the local authority would have to determine the charitable status of the organisation for rating purposes before the decision on registration has been made by the Charity Commission. Since rate relief cannot be claimed retrospectively in respect of previous rating periods, an organisation seeking registration as a charity, but which has not obtained registration, should put in a claim for rate relief before the end of any rating year; the local rating authority would then have to make its own determination, or more usually it would decide to defer a decision until the Charity Commission have reached their decision.

Where the organisation fails to be granted charitable status on the

grounds that, although some of its work is charitable, it is not established for charitable purposes only, it should first examine its constitution, and in particular its objects clause, to see whether this can be
amended to bring it within the charitable net; and secondly it might
consider the possibility of separating out its charitable activities and
putting these within a separate charitable trust, which would then
give an entitlement to rate relief. The rates position is not the only
factor and complex legal problems may be involved, but rate relief is
an important factor that should be taken into account in deciding
how the organisation is to be constituted and what activities it is
empowered to undertake.

4. Charities not entitled to mandatory rate relief

Certain charities are specifically excluded from entitlement to
mandatory rate relief (although this does not preclude them from
applying for and obtaining discretionary rate relief from their local
authority). These charities are listed in *Schedule 8* of the *1967
General Rate Act* (together with subsequent additions) and include
most universities (apart from Goldsmiths College London), insti-
tutes of postgraduate medical research (apart from the Institute of
Cancer Research), and colleges of science and technology.

Where an organisation finds itself in such a situation, it may wish
to consider the possibility of establishing an independent charitable
organisation for any charitable activities it is undertaking or intends
to undertake that can be separated out from its mainstream work.
For example if it runs a counselling service or a museum or a theatre,
these could (subject to the trusts attached to the charity property) be
constituted as separate independent charities and thereby become
eligible for mandatory rate relief. Obviously it will be simpler to do
this for an activity which is about to be established than where an
existing activity has to be transferred to the new trust; in the latter
case the Charity Commission's approval may well be needed and
perhaps there will be complex legal problems to be unravelled in
attempting to hive off from the charity some of its assets and
activities.

Discretionary rate relief

Once a charity (and in this context we include registered charities and also those non-registered organisations that are recognised as being charities by their local rating authority) has applied to the local rating authority in writing on the appropriate form, the rates that can be levied on any property occupied by the charity which is being used wholly or substantially for charitable purposes are reduced by 50 per cent from the amount that would otherwise be chargeable (except in Northern Ireland where 100 per cent mandatory relief is available). So the most that a charity will have to pay is half the rates bill. But this can still be a considerable sum.

The local rating authority also has the power to relieve the charity from some or all of the remaining 50 per cent of the rates that are chargeable. This power is conferred under *Section 40(5)* of the *1967 General Rate Act*. There is no obligation for the local rating authority to allow any charity any reduction beyond the mandatory 50 per cent. And policies and practices will vary from local authority to local authority.

The power to grant discretionary rate relief of up to 50 per cent is available for buildings or premises occupied by the following classes of organisation:

(a) Any charity entitled to mandatory rates relief;

(b) Any organisation established and operating on a not-for-profit basis, and whose main objects are charitable or are otherwise philanthropic or religious or concerned with education, social welfare, science, literature or the fine arts;

(c) Any club, society or other organisation established and operating on a not-for-profit basis, and wholly or mainly used for purposes of recreation.

It can readily be seen that discretionary relief may be given to many types of organisation that are not charities, and which are not entitled to mandatory rate relief.

Charities that are entitled to mandatory rate relief and other not-for-profit organisations that think they might fall into one of the other categories for which discretionary rate relief is available should apply to their local rating authority for discretionary rate relief. If they succeed, this will lead to a remission of all or part of

14

the 50 per cent of the rates bill that is within the power of the local rating authority to remit at its discretion under *Section 40(5)*.

The net effect is that up to 100 per cent rates relief may be available for charities and up to 50 per cent for certain other categories of organisation. It should be noted that discretionary relief is not an all or nothing affair; the local authority has the power to remit the whole of or only a proportion of the 50 per cent of the rates bill in the form of discretionary rate relief. It is more usual for the full 50 per cent discretionary rate relief to be granted where the authority decides to grant an organisation discretionary rate relief.

The cost of discretionary rate relief is borne locally by local ratepayers. Unlike mandatory rate relief, there is no central government grant to compensate the local rate fund for the cost of discretionary relief. Each local authority will have its own policies on the granting of discretionary relief. These policies will range from one extreme of automatically giving the full amount to any eligible organisation on application to the other extreme of refusing to do so under any circumstances. The first thing that an organisation seeking rate relief should do is to find out what (if any) policies exist for the area where its premises are situated. Assuming that it is possible to obtain some discretionary relief, the organisation should then apply for the full 50 per cent discretionary relief and use whatever lobbying it deems appropriate to further its cause.

The local authority may have a rule that the granting of discretionary relief depends on the level of local benefit that the organisation is providing; in which case the organisation should stress the benefit that it is actually providing within the local authority area, and if necessary keep the relevant statistics to demonstrate this. It might also be easier for a local authority to grant rate relief than it is for it to make a grant to the organisation; in that case the organisation can try to show that it is deserving of support and that the provision of discretionary rate relief is an extremely satisfactory way in which it might be supported. One point to note is that there is usually no connection between the decision-making process for making grants and the decision-making process for granting discretionary rate relief. They will usually be decided by different procedures and different committees within the local authority structure, and different criteria may be adopted when deciding which organisations to support. Just because an organisation has obtained a grant from its local authority, it does not automatically imply that it will obtain any discretionary rate relief.

An organisation considering relocating and setting up in a particular area may well want to discuss the rates situation with the local authority before coming to any decision – and indeed it has been known for local authorities to provide accommodation which are not only rates free but rent free, on the basis that the organisation will bring prestige or extra business to the area.

There are many arguments that an organisation can use, and each organisation will have to determine what works best in the particular circumstances. Even where discretionary relief is not granted, there is nothing to stop the organisation going back next year and in subsequent years to apply for discretionary relief. And if only a proportion of the full 50 per cent discretionary rate relief is granted, the charity may then go back to try to get an increase in the amount for subsequent years.

Discretionary relief can be granted for various periods of time. *Section 40(6)* of the *1967 General Rate Act* gives the local rating authority the power to grant relief for any of the following periods:

(a) For the rate year in which the decision is made, or for the rate year following;

(b) For a specified term of years not exceeding five, beginning not earlier than the rate year in which the decision is made or not more than 24 months from the date of the decision;

(c) For an indefinite period, beginning not earlier than the rate year in which the decision was made and subject to not less than 12 months' notice in writing of termination.

Thus the local rating authority might grant discretionary relief on a year-by-year basis, which would require the organisation to submit a fresh application each year. On the other hand, it is within the power of the local authority, and certainly in the interests of the organisation, for the relief to be granted on an indefinite basis. An organisation seeking discretionary rate relief might not only lobby its local authority to obtain the full 50 per cent relief that is available, but also to try to obtain the relief on an indefinite basis. It should be noted that as with mandatory relief, discretionary relief cannot be claimed retrospectively.

How the premises are used

There are two requirements, both of which must be met, for a charity to obtain either mandatory or discretionary rate relief:

    (a) The land and/or buildings must be occupied by an organisation which is determined to be a charity (for rating purposes); discretionary relief is also available for certain non-charitable organisations too, as specified in the previous section; and

    (b) The premises should be used wholly or mainly for charitable purposes.

This provides two further hurdles for a charity to overcome before it can obtain rate relief. Firstly it has to show that it is the actual occupier and not just the owner of the premises; and secondly it has to show that the premises are being used wholly or mainly for charitable purposes. Thus mandatory rate relief is not automatically given to any charity in respect of any land or buildings in its ownership. In most circumstances the situation will be clear cut. The premises either are or are not being occupied by the charity and used in the course of its charitable work. On occasions there may be circumstances where a charity will have to argue its case with its local rating authority, or even take the matter to appeal, if it feels that rate relief is due but is being unreasonably withheld. Here are some examples of where rate relief is available and where it is not:

A charity in occupation of premises in the course of its normal work will be entitled to obtain mandatory rate relief and it will be eligible to receive discretionary rate relief.

Even if the work the charity is undertaking in its occupation of the premises is not in a strict legal sense charitable − for example administration, selling Christmas cards (but not via a separate trading company), or fund-raising − but so long as this work is undertaken by the charity itself in the course of fulfilling its own charitable objectives, then rate relief will be available.

Where a caretaker resides in the premises and his doing so is of material significance to the work of the charity, then rate relief will be available on the caretaker's flat. In other circumstances rates would have to be paid on the caretaker's flat as it would not be deemed to be in use wholly or mainly for charitable purposes.

Where hostel or other accommodation is provided for individuals or families in need, then this will be deemed to be in fulfilment of the charity's objectives. But where the residents are paying a reasonable rent then the residents will be deemed to be the occupants and not the charity, and in consequence there will be no rate relief. Thus a registered fair rent (charitable) housing association will be able to claim rate relief on the premises it occupies for its administration, but not on the flats or houses it owns which are let or available for letting — in these cases the tenants (or licencees) will normally be deemed responsible for the rates, even where the housing association assumes the responsibility for collecting the rates. However, the situation is not always this simple. In the London Borough of Camden, two short-life housing associations (West Hampstead Housing Association and Short-Life Community Housing) both receive 100 per cent rate relief in respect of the dwellings occupied by their licencees, although a proper licence fee is charged; presumably this is granted on the basis that the licencees are in severe housing need or homeless, and the property is short-life housing and not permanent accommodation. The dividing line between what is a dwelling let out by the charity and what is a dwelling occupied by the charity in the course of its work is not clear cut. Whether or not rate relief will be available will depend on the terms of the tenancy or licence, the rent that is charged, the amount of caring services (if any) that are provided, and the attitude of the local authority.

Premises owned by the charity and let out as an investment will not be eligible for rate relief.

Premises used by the charity but occupied by a trading company which is wholly owned by the charity would not be eligible for rate relief. But if the trade were carried on directly by the charity and not via a separate trading company (*see section on Trading*), then rate relief would be available. Where a part of the premises (say, one floor) is used by the trading company, rate relief would not be available in respect of that part of the premises. There are separate provisions for charity shops (*see below*).

Premises occupied by a non-charitable campaigning wing of a charity would not be eligible for rate relief. For example 'War on Want' is entitled to rate relief on its offices but not in respect of that part of its offices occupied by 'WOW Campaigns' which is non-charitable. Similarly the 'Cobden Trust' can claim rate relief but the associated 'National Council of Civil Liberties' cannot.

Relief for charity shops

Special legislation exists for granting rate relief to charity shops. This was introduced following a test case in 1975 (*Oxfam v City of Birmingham*), where it was held that charity shops were not wholly or mainly used for charitable purposes, and therefore were not eligible for rate relief. The deciding point was that the getting in, raising or earning money for the charity was not itself a charitable activity, although the purpose for which the money was being raised was. Where a charity is undertaking these functions in conjunction with its other activities with which it shares premises, then those premises would fall within the 'wholly or mainly for charitable purposes' guideline. But where the activities were undertaken in separate premises, they would not be eligible for rate relief. Oxfam, which operated a large chain of charity shops, which as commercial premises would have had a high rate valuation, would have been particularly badly affected. The upshot was that new legislation to provide rate relief for charity shops was quickly introduced.

The *1976 Rating (Charity Shops) Act* provides that premises shall be deemed to be used wholly or mainly for charitable purposes if:

(a) It is used wholly or mainly for the sale of goods donated to a charity. The normal guideline is that over 50 per cent of turnover should arise from the sale of donated goods. The goods have to be donated to the charity for resale; where the goods are sold on commission and the charity is acting merely as a selling agent, the relief would not be granted. And

(b) All of the proceeds of the sale (after any deduction of expenses) are applied for the purposes of a charity. This means

19

in practice that the profits should be transferred each year to the charity's general funds. There may be instances of charity shops being established for the benefit of good cause projects which are not in fact charities – for example a local authority museum. In this case in order to gain eligibility for rate relief a museum development trust would have to be set up as a separate charity and the profits of the shop be applied to the charitable trust.

The shop may be run on a permanent basis in premises owned or leased for the purpose, or it may be run on a temporary basis in short-term premises. The rates situation is identical in either case. The shop may be owned and occupied by the charity itself or by a non-charitable trading company belonging to the charity or by a local supporters group or indeed by a commercial company; the ownership is irrelevant so long as both criteria are met – that the shop is selling mainly donated goods and that all of the profits arising are donated to a charity. Where a charity operates a number of shops, these criteria are applied to each individual shop operated by the charity. Even where the charity shops operated by the particular charity in total are selling more than 50 per cent donated goods, the fact that a particular shop is selling a lower amount of donated goods will disqualify that shop from eligibility for rate relief.

The *1976 Rating (Charity Shops) Act* gives the same rate relief as any charity premises, that is an entitlement to 50 per cent mandatory rate relief and the possibility of obtaining a further 50 per cent discretionary relief.

The only other circumstance in which a charity shop would be eligible for rate relief is when the shop itself is operated wholly or mainly for charitable purposes. This would then fall under the normal provisions for granting rate relief to charities in respect of premises occupied for charitable purposes. Where the production of the goods is a charitable activity (for example books and pamphlets on the issues that the charity is involved with, or goods made in sheltered workshops by the disabled people the charity has been set up to help), then the selling of those goods is an activity which directly helps fulfil the charity's objects, rather than one which provides only an indirect benefit via fund-raising. Determining whether or not a shop run by a charity is operating wholly or mainly for charitable purposes may not be clear-cut as some of the following examples indicate:

A development charity which runs projects for the relief of poverty in third world countries and sells the products produced by these projects would probably satisfy the 'wholly or mainly for charitable purposes' test. A similar shop selling goods produced in the countries in which it was active would not. There has to be a direct link between what is being sold and the beneficiaries of the charity.

A shop owned by a charity selling products from its disabled workshops would be eligible. Whereas the same shop, if it were selling products from disabled workshops not owned by the charity which is operating the workshops, would almost certainly not be entitled to rate relief.

An organisation set up to promote crafts activity might be eligible for rate relief on a shop selling craftworks located in the crafts centre on the basis that the resulting sales would help it fulfil its aims, but a crafts shop by itself could not set itself up as a charity and claim rate relief.

A shop run by a charity selling its own publications or other items it produces in the course of fulfilling its charitable objects (e.g. equipment for the blind, the deaf, the disabled) would be entitled to rate relief. An environmental bookshop run by an environmental organisation or a pet shop run by the RSPCA would not be entitled to rate relief.

These examples serve to show the general principles which exist in determining eligibility and where a charity finds that its claim for rate relief is being rejected it can always try to find similar instances where rate relief has been granted and try to persuade its local rating authority or take the matter to appeal.

Exemption from rates

The eligibility for rate relief depends on the status of the occupier (that they are a charity occupying the premises in the course of undertaking their charitable work). The nature of the use of the premises is a secondary factor which cannot by itself provide eligibility for rate relief. Thus a charity providing recreational facilities would be eligible for rate relief, whereas a commercial enterprise providing similar facilities would not. And a non-charitable but not-for-profit organisation providing the same facilities would be eligible for discretionary rate relief only.

There are certain circumstances when the occupier of a building will be exempted from paying rates. Unlike rate relief this will be determined by the use to which the building is being put rather than the charitable status of the occupier. The main categories of exemption which might be of relevance to voluntary organisations are: unoccupied property; places of religious worship; and certain institutions for the disabled.

Where an organisation is obtaining full rate relief on the premises it occupies, then it will not be paying rates and there will be little point in applying for an exemption. However, if the organisation is able to obtain only the 50 per cent mandatory rate relief and no further discretionary rate relief, it may be that the use to which the building is being put places it in a category where it is exempt from rates. And if the organisation can apply for and get an exemption, then no rates will be payable in respect of the exempt premises. Also, if the organisation is ineligible for rate relief because it is not a charity, it may still be eligible for an exemption.

The organisation occupying the building will need to notify the local rating authority of the use to which the building is being put and the fact that the premises should be exempted from rates in order to obtain the exemption. Without any such notification, the local authority will assume that the premises should be fully rated, and will charge the occupier accordingly.

Where an organisation is thinking of claiming an exemption from rates rather than applying for full rate relief, there is a tactical point which should be taken into consideration. Discretionary rate relief is granted to a charity at the discretion of the local authority. When the local authority is reviewing the support it is giving to local voluntary organisations it may aggregate the grants and the rate reliefs it is making available. An exemption from rates is a right which depends on the use to which the premises are being put, and it will not show up in any figures for the support given to voluntary organisations that the local authority might compile. And obtaining exemption from rates rather than rate relief may make it easier for an applicant organisation to obtain a larger grant or maintain the level of grant it is getting from its local authority.

There are three main categories for rates exemption which concern charities:

1. Unoccupied buildings

Certain categories of unoccupied building are exempted from rates. This provision applies to any owner regardless of whether they have charitable status or not. Since the *1967 General Rate Act* empty property rate relief is not an automatic right. Any organisation faced with a rates demand for a building that is not occupied should seek to ascertain whether empty property relief can be obtained.

2. Places of religious worship

Under *Section 39* of the *1967 General Rate Act* places of public religious worship are exempt from rates. The application of this section is limited to bona fide religious bodies and cannot be extended to any organisation simply because it claims to be a religion and that it is using the premises for public worship. For the purpose of this exemption, the following are defined as being places of public religious worship:

(a) Any place of public religious worship which belongs to the established Churches or which is certified as required by law as being a place of religious worship.

(b) Any ancillary church hall, chapel hall or similar building used for the purposes of the organisation responsible for the conduct of public religious worship at that place.

3. Institutions for the disabled

Under *Section 2* of the *1978 Rating (Disabled Persons) Act* the occupier of buildings is granted a rates rebate equal to the whole of the rates chargeable (that is no rates will be payable) when the buildings are used wholly for the following purposes (or partly for the purposes and partly for ancillary purposes):

(a) The provision of residential accommodation for the care of persons suffering from illness or the after-care of persons who have been suffering from illness. Care specifically excludes the provision of medical, surgical or dental treatment. And illness is as defined in *Section 128(1)* of the *1977 National Health Service Act* as including mental disorder within the meaning of the *1959 Mental Health Act* or any injury or disability requiring medical or dental treatment or nursing.

(b) The provision of facilities for training or keeping suitably occupied persons suffering from illness or persons who have been suffering from illness (again as defined in the NHS Act).

(c) The provision of residential accommodation and facilities as in (a) and (b) for disabled persons.

(d) The provision of welfare services for disabled persons of a kind which the local authority has the power to provide under *Section 29* of the *1948 National Assistance Act*.

(e) The provision of a workshop or other facilities under *Section 15* of the *1944 Disabled Persons (Employment) Act* and *Section 3(1)* of the *1958 Disabled Persons (Employment) Act*.

Section 1 of the *1978 Rating (Disabled Persons) Act* provides partial rebates in respect of special facilities in dwellings needed because of the disability of a person who is normally resident. And subsequent sections of the Act provide similar rebates for Scotland.

The provisions of the *1978 Rating (Disabled Persons) Act* are far less well known than the entitlement to rate relief. One reason is that it is a recent piece of legislation; another perhaps is that where the occupant of the building is a charity, they might be receiving full rate relief and therefore see no necessity to apply for a rate rebate. However the difference is that the institution (which may or may not be a charity) is entitled to a full rebate when it uses the premises for one of the specified purposes, whereas it is entitled only to 50 per cent rate relief as of right and the remaining 50 per cent is at the discretion of the local authority; and even if granted in full, this discretionary relief may be withdrawn or discontinued subsequently.

A further different is the cost to the local rating authority. If the premises are granted the full 100 per cent rate relief, the cost of this will be shared by central government and the local authority, with the 50 per cent discretionary relief being paid for out of local funds. Under the *1978 Rating (Disabled Persons) Act*, any rebate granted by the local authority is reimbursed by central government to the tune of 90 per cent. The remaining 10 per cent is written off as a loss on collection by the local rating authority, and is therefore paid for out of local funds. So although there is no difference to the charity between full rate relief and a rebate under this Act, the rate rebate will be the cheaper option as far as the local authority is concerned as it can recoup a greater proportion of the cost from central government.

The 90 per cent grant is paid under *Section 69* of the *1980 Local Government Planning and Land Act*. If the Department of the Environment considers that the rebate has been improperly granted, then it has the power to stop the 90 per cent grant. In this case the whole of the cost of the rebate would be borne out of local funds. Because the 1978 Act is so new, there is very little case law as yet and the Act is being interpreted in a variety of ways by local rating authorities. The problems have mainly arisen with *Section 2* in relation to institutional ratepayers, rather than *Section 1* which covers the domestic side and is working well. Towards the end of 1982 the Department of the Environment will review the operation of the Act in consultation with the local authority associations with a view to giving clearer guidance on the application of the Act or, if necessary, promoting amending legislation to correct the numerous anomalies that have arisen.

The problems in interpretation can be illustrated by the following case. In 1982 the 'Church of England Children's Society' successfully obtained a full rebate under the Act in respect of a school for maladjusted boys on the basis that it was providing facilities for the training and keeping suitably occupied of the mentally ill. The Society had appealed in the County Court against a rate demand from the London Borough of Southwark which had not given full discretionary rate relief on the premises.

The Department of the Environment's view of the interpretation of 'training' for special schools is that: 'Training as in *Section 2(2)(b)* of the Act denotes training in manual skills as opposed to education which is training of the mind. Thus training as in *Section 2(2)(b)* excludes education and hence special schools'. Although this interpretation is arguable and indeed the County Court took a different view, until a higher court gives judgement the Department retains this view. In the view of the Department the Southwark Case should have gone to appeal, but Southwark had little incentive to take the matter to appeal when it could get reimbursement of 90 per cent of the cost of the rebate from central government. However the Department is only bound by judgements in a higher court and could therefore refuse to pay the 90 per cent grant in this instance.

In most cases an organisation will clearly fall inside or outside the provisions of the 1978 Act and will not encounter any legal problems. And even where the situation is not clear cut, the local authority might be prepared to interpret the Act quite liberally to cover the premises occupied by the organisation and to give a rebate. This is something positive that the local authority can do to help charities in their area at little cost to themselves; although how far they can go will be constrained by whether they can obtain reimbursement from central government.

There are two circumstances where an eligible charity might apply for a rebate:

(a) Where it is not able to obtain 100 per cent rate relief; or

(b) Even where it is obtaining 100 per cent rate relief, since a rebate will result in a lower cost to local ratepayers.

Because the Act is new and not widely known as yet, charities which work with the sick, the disabled, the convalescent or the mentally ill should consider the provisions of the Act and whether they might be eligible, particularly where they are unable to obtain full rate relief. The following instance illustrates the benefits of doing this.

'City Roads (Crisis Intervention)' applied to the London Borough of Islington for full rate relief as a charity. Due to the large number of charities active in the Borough the Borough's policy was one of giving only 50 per cent mandatory rate relief. In 1982 the charity wrote to the Finance Officer referring to the *1978 Rating (Disabled Persons) Act* arguing that as a medical unit dealing with a social

26

disability (drug addiction) which undertakes detoxification programmes, this qualified under the Act as providing accommodation,
relief and training for disabled persons. This was accepted by the
Council as qualifying for a full rate rebate, which was then granted.

So if you feel that you are likely to qualify for a rebate and if you
are not receiving the full 100 per cent rate relief, it will be well worth
asking for a rate rebate under this Act. And even if you feel that
there is only a slim chance that you might qualify it might still be
worth approaching your local authority.

Action points

The rates bill that a charity faces is not the most important item of
expenditure in its budget; but it can be significant and it is worth
getting the situation sorted out to the charity's advantage. It will
save money now and it will save money in the future; and it is far
simpler to take advantage of the available reliefs than it is to raise an
equivalent amount of money.

The first step is to ascertain what rates the charity is paying – to
see what is attracting full rate relief, what is attracting mandatory
relief only, what has been granted an exemption, and where full
rates are being paid. Once this basic information has been got
together, there are several main areas where the organisation might
look to reduce its rates bill; and the sooner any action is taken the
better, as rate relief cannot be claimed retrospectively.

(a) A charity in receipt of mandatory relief should do all it can to
'persuade' its local authority to grant it the full 50 per cent
discretionary relief, if it is not already getting this.

(b) A charity in receipt of rate relief in respect of only a part of its
premises should examine whether it can mount an argument
that more of the premises it occupies should be granted rate
relief.

(c) Any organisation working with the ill or the disabled, if it
fails to be granted any rate relief on account of the fact that it
is non-charitable, or if it is a charity and fails to obtain full

27

discretionary relief from its local authority, should examine whether it can get a full rate rebate on the premises.

(d) A non-profit organisation which has not obtained charitable status should see whether it can obtain charitable status for rating purposes from its local authority or whether it can obtain discretionary relief even if it is not entitled to mandatory relief.

(e) An organisation not entitled to mandatory rate relief (including non-charities and excluded charities) should see whether any particular project which is run for charitable purposes only could be hived off as a separate charity which would be entitled to rate relief.

(f) A charity shop which fails to meet the criteria for rate relief should examine its trading policy, particularly if the rates bill is a significant item of cost.

(g) An organisation seeking registration as a charity should apply for rate relief at the earliest opportunity, and not wait for a determination of its charitable status from the Charity Commission (or the Inland Revenue where appropriate). Rate relief cannot be granted retrospectively in respect of previous rating years.

It should be noted that some local authorities are prepared to interpret their powers for granting rate relief and rate rebates quite liberally and even go beyond the letter (and the spirit) of the law in an attempt to help charities. The fact that a particular charity has been granted relief on permanent market stalls let out commercially or a rebate on an old people's housing scheme (both actual cases), does not create a precedent for other charities in other areas. A knowledge of how 'lenient' the local authority is likely to be in its 'interpretation' of its powers is important in assessing the chances of obtaining relief or a rebate in marginal circumstances. And when in doubt, a charity should apply rather than not apply.

In addition and in common with any ratepayer a charity should see whether the rateable value of the premises it is occupying can be reduced. This will only be worth considering if the organisation is not receiving full 100 per cent rate relief. The fact that the occupier is a charity does not now affect the rateable value of the premises occupied, although as we have seen this was the only way in which charities could get rate relief earlier this century.

Any ratepayer is entitled to challenge the valuation list by proposing an alteration. This is done on a form obtainable from the local Valuation Office of the Inland Revenue (which is responsible for determining rateable values). There is a statutory period of four months during which the Valuation Officer and the ratepayer can attempt to seek agreement. If after that period the matter is still in dispute, the appeal is forwarded by the Valuation Office to the Local Valuation Panel for determination by the Local Valuation Court which is an independent tribunal. There is also a right to appeal against the decision of the Local Valuation Court to the Lands Tribunal, provided that the ratepayer attended or was represented at the Local Valuation Court. It is part of the basic structure of the rating system that if you improve your property, say by installing central heating, you thereby increase the notional rental value and therefore its rateable value. But equally if there is any loss of amenity since the valuation list was last completed, you might qualify for a reduction in rateable value − for example, more traffic on the roads resulting from new development subsequent to the previous assessment of rateable value (in 1973) may have increased the level of ambient noise and danger. If a charity thinks that it has a good case for whatever reasons, then there is nothing to stop it attempting to get the rateable value of its premises reduced.

2. Salaries

The important tax concession available to charities in the area of staff costs is relief from Employers National Insurance Surcharge. There are several other areas where charities can obtain benefit in respect of staff remuneration:

1. Manpower Services Commission schemes

The MSC runs special programmes for the unemployed. One programme that has been aimed particularly at charities is the Community Programme. This is aimed at the longer-term unemployed (18–24 year olds who have been unemployed for 6 months, and over 25s who have been unemployed for at least a year). Sponsors are reimbursed up to a maximum of £60 per place per week for creating full and part-time job opportunities. The programme aims to provide 130,000 places. There is also the Voluntary Projects Programme which aims to promote adult education and community activity for the unemployed. Organisations setting up projects to recruit unemployed volunteers under this scheme can claim up to £6,400 for their paid staff to run the project as well as money for premises costs and equipment; there is a maximum of £75,000 per scheme and the budget for the programme is £8 million. The MSC's policies and programmes for the unemployed are in a continual state of flux and charities should consult with their local Council of Voluntary Service or MSC office to see what is available and how (if at all) they might benefit.

2. Secondments from industry

Some firms make available some of their staff to help charities. In some cases this is done informally; in a few companies there is a positive attempt to match up their own personnel development

31

policies with the needs of charities. Secondments can be made on a very part-time basis, for say a few hours a week, where someone with a particular skill (book-keeping, marketing, etc.) assists the charity. There are schemes for sabbaticals and mid-career management development, when someone is placed with a charity for between 6 months and a year. There are schemes using people in the latter stages of their working life in the run-up to retirement as an alternative to early retirement or redundancy. There are post-retirement schemes, particularly those co-ordinated by the Retired Executives Action Clearing House (Victoria House, Southampton Row, London WC1). If a charity feels it can benefit from a full-time or part-time secondment, it should make its needs known to the particular company or agency which might be able to help.

3. Volunteers

This is an area where charities have traditionally drawn support to undertake 'good works'. It is something that government seeks to encourage, but it has diminished in importance amongst some voluntary agencies as they have sought to professionalise the services they offer, and because the idea of self-help by individuals and communities to the problems they face has grown at the expense of the idea of 'do-gooding'. But volunteering is still an important source of help for many charities and volunteers are able to undertake a wide variety of tasks from taking out old people, running a hospital library service, manning a thrift shop, teaching language or literacy, visiting prisoners, cleaning up a canal or creating a neighbourhood park. There are Volunteer Bureaux and other specialised agencies promoting and co-ordinating volunteer work up and down the country. A volunteer normally works for free. But a charity may wish to reimburse expenses or even pay a small honorarium.

Where a volunteer is unemployed and in receipt of benefit, certain conditions will have to be met if benefit is not to be lost. In most circumstances a person's voluntary work will not affect his entitlement to benefit, but there are occasions when it can. One of the conditions for receiving Unemployment Benefit, and Supplementary Benefit when unemployed, is that a person must be available for work. To be 'available for work' means that the person must be able straightaway to go for a job or for an interview. However, a person can be treated as available for work when undertaking voluntary work, even though he is not in fact so, in the following circumstances:

(a) For any day on which he provides a service which he is unable to give up immediately, so long as he can drop it given 24 hours' notice;

(b) When he is away from home attending a work camp in Great Britain run by a charity or local authority. In this case he can be treated as being available for work when he is away for one period only of up to a maximum of 14 days (excluding Sundays) in any calendar year; but if he is to be away he must tell the Unemployment Benefit Office in advance when and where he is going;

(c) When he is working as a member of an organised group in an emergency.

If the voluntary work done is paid, other rules will have to be satisfied if benefit is not to be lost. For any day on which the person works he must remain free to take a full-time job; he must not earn more than £2 a day (certain expenses can be allowed); and he must not work in his usual main job, unless he is working for a charity, a local authority or a health authority.

A leaflet (*N.I.240*) is available from the DHSS explaining how various benefits are affected by voluntary work.

National Insurance Surcharge

National Insurance Surcharge is payable under the *1976 National Insurance Surcharge Act* in respect of Class I National Insurance Contributions which are payable in respect of employed staff. National Insurance Surcharge does not form part of the National Insurance income, but is a tax which is collected with the Employers' National Insurance Contributions purely as a matter of convenience. The proceeds are paid into the Treasury Fund and not the National Insurance Fund. The Department of Health and Social Security is the government department responsible for the assessment and collection of National Insurance contributions, including National Insurance Surcharge.

SALARIES

Under *Section 57* of the *1977 Finance Act* a charity is exempted from paying the National Insurance Surcharge. The current rate of Employers' National Insurance Contribution (excluding the Surcharge) is 10.2 per cent (not contracted-out rate) or 5.7 per cent (contracted-out rate). The current rate of the Surcharge is $2\frac{1}{2}$ per cent. The benefit to the charity of this exemption is therefore $2\frac{1}{2}$ per cent of its total salary and wages bill.

These figures relate to 1983–84 and subsequently. Prior to 5th April 1982 the rate of the Employers' National Insurance Surcharge was $3\frac{1}{2}$ per cent. For 1982–83 as a transitional measure because of the difficulty of adjusting the payments, the rate was held at $3\frac{1}{2}$ per cent from 6th April to 1st August 1982 and reduced to 2 per cent for the period 2nd August 1982 to 5th April 1983; this resulted in an average rate of just less than $2\frac{1}{2}$ per cent for the whole year.

Relief from National Insurance Surcharge is a relatively small concession for charities but nonetheless it is well worth having. On a salary bill of £30,000 per annum the value of the relief is £750 per annum. It should be noted that this relief can only be claimed in respect of employees of the charity. It will not apply to any self-employed person working for the charity, nor will it apply to employees of a trading company owned and operated by the charity.

Organisations will only be entitled to receive this relief if they have charitable status − that is if they are registered with the Charity Commission, or if they fall within one of the categories excused registration and have been determined to be charitable by the Inland Revenue.

For a new organisation that is in the process of applying for charitable status but which has not yet received charitable status, where the organisation is already employing staff it will have to pay its Employers' National Insurance Contributions at the full rate. However, when its charitable status comes through, it can then make a claim for a rebate in respect of the Surcharge it has paid prior to receiving charitable status. On receipt of charitable status the objects of the organisation have been determined as being wholly charitable. If there has been no significant change in the nature of the organisation since it was established up until the date that it received charitable status, the Inland Revenue will accept that it was a charity operating 'for charitable purposes only' prior to receiving its charitable status, and therefore entitled to exemption from the Surcharge.

SALARIES

Similarly if a charity has inadvertently been paying its Employers' National Insurance Contributions at the full rate, as soon as this is discovered it should not only start paying at the reduced rate but it should also put in a claim for a rebate in respect of the excess contributions it has already made. It is surprising how often charities are not aware of this concession, and it pays to check that the contributions are being paid at the reduced rate.

It is for the Inland Revenue (Claims Branch) to decide whether an organisation is entitled to exemption from the Surcharge and whether it is also entitled to a refund in respect of any Surcharge already paid. The Department of Health and Social Security in effect acts as an agent in collection of the tax. Any request for exemption or claims for a refund should be addressed to the Department of Health and Social Security. The Department of Health and Social Security have an administrative arrangement with the Inland Revenue which enables them to make a refund of any National Insurance Surcharge paid by a charity where this is due, and a subsequent credit is made to the National Insurance Fund from the Treasury in respect of any refunds made. Any queries regarding refunds should be made to the Department of Health and Social Security, Newcastle-upon-Tyne, NE98 1YU.

The National Insurance Surcharge is one of the more hated fiscal devices. It is seen by industry as a tax on employment and something which helps make British companies uncompetitive. Each year in the months leading up to the budget a vigorous campaign is mounted to have the tax abolished. Up until 1982 the Chancellor stood his ground, and prior to 1982 the only change that was made since the Surcharge was introduced in 1976 was to raise it from 2 per cent to $3\frac{1}{2}$ per cent in October 1978. At the time of writing the indications are that the Surcharge will be further reduced in 1983. But it should be noted that if the Surcharge were to be abolished, this would help industry but it would not help charities, since they are already exempted from paying it.

3. Individual giving

One aspect of charitable status which should not be underestimated is the seal of approval that is implied by having such status. 'If it is charitable, it must be worthwhile'. But there are two quite different aspects of the word 'charity'. The first is a strict legal definition of a body which is eligible for a wide range of tax reliefs. The second has connotations of being an organisation that is worthwhile and worthy of support. Despite the fact that being a charity gives no guarantee that the organisation has objects that are relevant to the world of today, or that it is well run and effective in what it does, or even that the motives of its promoters are benevolent, being a charity is of considerable help in fund-raising beyond any actual benefits conferred by the legal status of the organisation.

But the tax concessions which a charity enjoys and which it can take advantage of in its fund-raising are also extremely important. In this section we will look at:

(a) Gifts of income made by a donor under Deed of Covenant;

(b) Gifts of capital made by a donor on his death and during his lifetime;

(c) Gifts in kind;

(d) The possibility for charities to collect money from the public in public places.

Covenants

A Deed of Covenant is a legal agreement by a donor to make regular (usually annual) payments out of his income to a beneficiary. It is a binding legal obligation which makes over the legal title to certain income to a beneficiary for the period of the covenant. In order to be valid it should not be a payment for goods or services received by the donor. It must also be irrevocable, that is it can only be terminated with the consent of the beneficiary. If the donor defaults, the charity could sue the donor for those covenant payments not received. However, failure of the covenant to run its full term (as a result of default) will not make those covenant payments already received ineligible for tax relief, provided that it was the intention of both the donor and the beneficiary at the outset that the covenant should run for its full term.

For a covenant made in favour of a charity, under *Section 360* of the *1970 Taxes Act* the charity is relieved from paying Income Tax on any annual payments it receives under covenant. If the donor pays Income Tax and pays the covenant out of his net taxed income, the charity is entitled to recover the Income Tax paid by the donor at the basic rate. In addition the donor, if he pays Income Tax at a higher rate, is entitled to offset his covenant payments as a deductible expense against the higher rate tax he pays. This higher rate tax relief is available for £3,000 of (gross) covenanted income, which is equivalent to £2,100 of (net) covenant payments made by the donor, with the basic rate of Income Tax currently at 30 per cent. If the donor does not pay Income Tax on his income, when he makes his covenant payment 'after deduction of Income Tax at the basic rate', he will be obliged at the same time to pay Income Tax calculated at the basic rate in respect of his net covenant payment to the Inland Revenue, and this Income Tax can then be reclaimed by the charity; alternatively if he cannot provide evidence that he has paid tax at the basic rate, then the charity will not be able to reclaim any tax in respect of the covenant payment. And in these circumstances there is no additional benefit to the charity of the donation being made under Deed of Covenant.

The minimum period for a covenant made in favour of a charity is now four years. In order to obtain the tax relief, the first requirement for the organisation is that it will need to provide evidence that it is a charity. Registration with the Charity Commission is automatic proof of charitable status; but for those charities in Scotland and Northern Ireland where no registration procedure exists and for those charities exempted or excused from registration, their charitable status will be determined by the Inland Revenue when processing their claim to recover the tax. A new charity in the process of registering cannot reclaim any tax on its covenant income until it is actually registered, but it can make a retrospective claim relating to any covenant income it received prior to registration (on the basis that it was operating for charitable purposes only and therefore a charity prior to registration). The normal procedure is that a claim for tax repayment has to be made within six years of the end of the tax year in which the covenant payment was made, if the tax is to be repaid by the Inland Revenue.

A second requirement is that the covenanted payment must be applied for charitable purposes by the charity, and the charity must show if it is called to do so that it is not just accumulating the money for no particular purpose. A third requirement is that the donor must be paying Income Tax at the basic rate (currently 30 per cent); the donor has to sign a Certificate of Deduction of Tax (under a special scheme designed to reduce the administrative work of the Inland Revenue this is required in the first year only for net covenant payments of £130 or less). Fourthly the charity has to make a claim to the Claims Branch of the Inland Revenue in respect of the tax paid which it wishes to recover. This has to be done in a set manner using forms provided for the purpose.

A covenant is a precise legal document which needs to be worded and filled in in the correct manner. Although this procedure for reclaiming tax might appear quite complicated, it is in fact relatively easy to draw up a specimen form (perhaps using the wording from another charity's) and processing these in the required manner. If even this is too difficult, the Charities Aid Foundation offer a service for administering covenants on behalf of charities at modest cost.

The advantages of covenanted income are well worth having:

(a) Giving under covenant increases the value of a donation to the charity by 42.8 per cent at the current 30 per cent basic rate of Income Tax.

(b) A covenant encourages a donor to give over a longer period of time (the period of a covenant now has to be four years or longer) and there is always the possibility of getting a renewal when the covenant expires. The length of time that a covenant runs and the long-term commitment to the charity that is required is a slight deterrent to donors; and the intention of the 1980 Finance Act in reducing the minimum period of a covenant to four years was to encourage donors.

39

INDIVIDUAL GIVING

(c) Higher Rate Relief makes it attractive for a high rate taxpayer to give in this way. The cost per annum to a higher rate tax-payer of giving a £10 covenant to charity is shown in the table below. (The charity will receive £14.28 after reclaiming tax in each case.)

Tax Rate	Cost of £10 covenant
30%	£10.00
40%	£8.57
45%	£7.86
50%	£7.14
55%	£6.43
60%	£5.71
65%	£5.00
70%	£4.29
75%	£3.57

Covenants are a major tax concession to charities, which can provide a stimulus for people to give to charity. The 1980 Finance Act, which introduced higher rate relief and shortened the minimum period of a covenant made to a charity, was an attempt by governments to support charitable activity at a time of severe constraints on public spending. All the incentives are there for charities to make the most of this opportunity. At present the covenanted donations and subscriptions received by charity amount to around £150 million, and the tax relief enjoyed by charities amounts to 30 per cent of this. This is a significant part of the £500 million that the Charities Aid Foundation estimates that charities receive in donations from individuals and the £50 million in company giving, most of which is under Deed of Covenant (1980–81 figures). But at the same time it has the potential to be expanded, and charities should seize the opportunity and sell the benefits of giving under covenant to their supporters.

For a much more detailed account of covenanted giving, see the companion publication to this, 'Covenants: a practical guide to the *tax advantages of giving'*, and this is available from the Directory of Social Change (9 Mansfield Place, London NW3 1HS). The Charities Aid Foundation (48 Pembury Road, Tonbridge, Kent TN9 2JD) produce a pamphlet on covenant administration and provide a number of services to donors and charities for covenant giving.

Gifts of capital

There are three circumstances in which gifts of capital might be received by a charity, each with its own tax considerations: gifts during a donor's lifetime, legacies and bequests on the death of the donor, and large donations made in the form of loan-covenants (also known as deposited covenants). Each of these will be considered in this section. In addition we will also examine the possibilities for making gifts in kind rather than in cash and the savings in Capital Gains Tax that might accrue as a result.

Capital Transfer Tax is levied on gifts made by individuals during their lifetime and on death. Tax is levied on the cumulative total of all transfers made after 26th March 1974 during the lifetime of the individual after deducting exempt transfers, together with all property passing on death. The rate of tax levied increases progressively with the amount given away, rising up to a maximum level of 75 per cent.

The tax starts on cumulative transfers in excess of £55,000. There are different rates payable on transfers made during the donor's lifetime and on transfers made on death or three years prior to death. The tax rates and the tax bands as from April 1982 are indexed with the rate of inflation unless and until Parliament decides otherwise. Capital Transfer Tax is administered by the Capital Taxes Office of the Inland Revenue, to whom any queries should be addressed.

Certain transfers are exempt from the tax. The main exemptions are firstly for gifts up to a maximum of £3,000 from any one individual in any Income Tax year, and secondly and in addition to this, gifts up to a total of £250 per recipient in any Income Tax year.

But charities enjoy important exemptions from this Tax on gifts received by them during the donor's lifetime and on his death. This makes giving capital to charity attractive particularly for those individuals whose wealth is substantial.

Gifts to charity made by a donor out of his income are not subject to Capital Transfer Tax at all. The donor may have to satisfy the Inland Revenue that the gift was part of his normal pattern of expenditure – that it was made out of his income, and that having made the gift he still had sufficient income remaining to maintain his accustomed lifestyle; otherwise the gift may be treated as a capital transfer. A covenanted gift is normally a gift made out of income, since there is a clear intention that this will be a recurring item of expenditure; and a donation made in this way has clear tax advantages over a one-time gift made out of income or a capital gift. **Wherever possible a donor should be encouraged to give out of income, either under Deed of Covenant or with a loan-covenant arrangement**; the value of the gift as a result will be increased by 42.8 per cent, where the donor pays Income Tax at the basic rate, and the donor may also be eligible for Higher Rate Relief.

All gifts are welcome to a charity in need of funds, but where possible a donor should be encouraged to give in the most tax-effective way. The circumstances in which a capital gift becomes attractive as compared with a gift made out of income under Deed of Covenant are:

(a) Where a donor wishes to make a very large gift which cannot reasonably be made out of his income, even under a loan-covenant arrangement;

(b) Where the donor's expectation of life is such that he may not live to see a covenant run its full term, although the reduction to four years means that this will be far less of a problem;

(c) Where a donor wishes to transfer more than £250,000 of his assets to charity; this is best done where any excess over £250,000 is given as a lifetime gift, rather than leaving the whole of the money as a bequest;

(d) Where the donor wishes to transfer property, stocks and shares or other gifts in kind, where there may be some advantage in terms of relief from Capital Gains Tax, although the tax advantage will never be as great as if the asset were sold and the proceeds donated under covenant;

(e) Bequests and legacies made on death, where the donor might not be prepared to make an equivalent gift during his lifetime. And legacies are often neglected as a source of income that a charity might plan to raise.

1. Lifetime capital gifts

For charities obtaining gifts of capital from individual donors during the lifetime of the donor, there is an important exemption from tax. Gifts to charities are completely exempt from Capital Transfer Tax, providing the following three conditions are met:

(a) The charity is established in the UK and the gift is applied for charitable purposes;

(b) The gift is unconditional. The exemption does not apply for gifts made for a limited period or where less than the full interest in the property is transferred. Where the gift is conditional on some future event, that condition should be satisfied within twelve months of the gift being made for the exemption to apply.

(c) The gift is made *more than one year before the donor's death*; this condition was introduced to prevent avoidance by deathbed transfers.

There is one potential problem for a charity in receipt of a lifetime gift. It is in the donor's power to determine that the gift shall be made to a UK charity and applied for charitable purposes only, and also that it shall be unconditional; however, it is not in his power to determine that he shall live for more than one year after the gift has been made. If he should die within one year of making the gift, the gift is aggregated with other charitable gifts made during the last year of his life and all charitable bequests made on death, and if this total should exceed £250,000, the charity may become liable to pay Capital Transfer Tax. This £250,000 limit does not include gifts made to certain exempt beneficiaries which are completely free of Capital Transfer Tax (*see section on Legacies*). The amount of tax to be paid is a complicated sum to calculate, and will depend on a number of factors including the value of the estate, the amount of taxable transfers made during the person's lifetime, and the value of the transfers to charity in the last year of life and on death. The sum assessed to tax is the value of the gift only, and not the amount received grossed up at the appropriate rate of Capital Transfer Tax.

It should be remembered that this contingent liability only exists if the donor makes more than £250,000 of gifts to charity in the last year of life and on death. If the charity receives only a small donation from a donor whose scale of philanthropy may push him over the magic £250,000 mark, should the donor die within twelve months, then the contingent liability to the charity will not be that great; and should any Capital Transfer Tax become due, it could quite simply be paid out of normal revenues.

There may be problems with substantial gifts made by a donor who has given or intends to give very substantially in the twelve months prior to or following the gift being made to the charity, or who intends to make substantial charitable bequests on his death, and here the recipient charity may need to take some action. It may be that the gift will remain unspent at the time of the donor's death and there will be sufficient funds to meet any Capital Transfer Tax liability, should it arise. The Inland Revenue have an Extra-Statutory Concession (F3) to waive payment of the tax where the money has been spent and where there are no funds available to meet the claim. But this is a concession and not a right, and the action of the Inland Revenue will depend on the particular circumstances. Where charities are not incorporated with limited liability, the trustees would be personally liable to meet the claim, should this be pursued and the charity have no funds; and even where the tax can be paid, a hard-won donation will have been partly frittered away. This serves to put into perspective the need for a charity in receipt of a substantial gift to take some sort of precautionary action.

There are two steps a charity can take. The first is to sound out the donor about the scale of his giving and whether he intends to leave a great deal to charity on his death. All the charity needs to know is whether it is at risk. And then if it finds itself in the position where the death of the donor would result in a tax liability, it can either hold some or all of the money on deposit for twelve months or take out an insurance on the donor's life.

Where a charity is in receipt of a gift that is conditional, there may be the possibility that all the conditions will not be met within twelve months and that the gift will thereby fall outside the exemption from Capital Transfer Tax. The charity might advise the donor to make the gift in some other way in order to avoid the possibility of having to pay Capital Transfer Tax:

(a) The gift could be deferred until such a time as it is certain that all conditions can be met within twelve months or until the gift can be made unconditionally;

(b) The money can be given in the form of an interest-free loan, until such a time that all the conditions that the donor requires are met, at which time it can be converted into a gift.

The sort of situation in which this is likely to arise is where a charity receives a gift for the second stage of a building project or to provide for the running costs subsequently, and the gift is conditional on the building works being completed. A delay in the building programme could affect the exemption from Capital Transfer Tax.

The exemptions for charities only apply to charities established in the UK. Gifts to non-charities and to external charities are subject to Capital Transfer Tax in the same way as any gift made to an individual. The exemptions would allow the recipient to receive a maximum sum of £3,000 from an individual donor in any tax year free of Capital Transfer Tax, provided that no other gift of more than £250 was made to anyone else in the same tax year.

2. Legacies and bequests

Gifts made to charities within one year of death, together with the total of all legacies and bequests made to charities upon death are exempt up to a total of £250,000, provided that the charities receiving the gifts are established in the UK and the gifts are to be applied for charitable purposes. Included in this total will be any loans made to charities where repayment is waived on the death of the lender under the terms of the loan. This situation may, in particular, apply for loans outstanding as part of a loan-covenant arrangement.

Gifts made to certain beneficiaries, whether on death or before death, are completely exempt. These include most national, local authority and university museums and galleries, university libraries, any university or university college in the UK, any government department or local authority, and certain specified charities, including the National Trust and Scottish National Trust, the National Art Collections Fund, the Historic Churches Preservation Trust, the Nature Conservancy Council, and the Friends of the National Libraries. Gifts to exempt beneficiaries are not included in the £250,000 exemption limit.

Many people are only prepared to give substantially to charity upon their death. This is partly because of an innate fear of having to live out their last days in poverty, partly because the high rate of Capital Transfer Tax on large estates makes this an attractive proposition, and partly because of a wish to redeem themselves by doing good (the pagoda building syndrome, where the number of pagodas you build determines your place in heaven).

The total legacy income obtained by all charities in 1981 was estimated as £260 million, which represented 10 per cent of their total income. The top 12 charities for legacy income (Source: Charities Aid Foundation) were:

Imperial Cancer Research Fund	£8.17 million
Cancer Research Campaign	£7.02 million
National Trust	£5.10 million
Dr Barnardo's	£5.01 million
Royal National Lifeboat Institution	£4.88 million
RSPCA	£4.79 million
Royal National Institute for the Blind	£4.04 million
Salvation Army	£3.00 million
People's Dispensary for Sick Animals	£2.94 million
Guide Dogs for the Blind	£2.06 million
Leonard Cheshire Foundation	£1.78 million
Arthritis and Rheumatism Council	£1.67 million

Some charities are seemingly very successful at obtaining legacies. In some cases there are obvious reasons. Charities concerned with terminal disease and with the results of ageing, and animal charities, do extremely well. But a key factor to success is deciding that you want to get legacy income and then doing something about it. Some of the ways in which charities set about getting legacy income include:

(a) Advertising this possibility to their members and supporters and encouraging them to make a bequest;

(b) Advertising to solicitors who often act as advisers when people draw up a Will through the various yearbooks and journals; there are three main media that charities use: *Will to Charity*, the *Law Society's Gazette*, and the *Family Welfare Association's Directory of Social Services*; the *Solicitor's Journal* and the *New Law Journal* also both produce charity supplements which contain legacy advertising;

(c) Generally keeping a high profile with the public, in particular through press advertising.

One problem is the time-scale involved. Most charities need support NOW. When getting legacies, effort will be rewarded several years on; and money will have to be spent now to persuade supporters to make a bequest, which the charity will not recover for perhaps five years. So legacy income is long-term income, and any charity wishing to get money from this source should think well ahead and not wait until it is in financial crisis to do something.

Getting legacy income is like any other form of fund-raising. The charity has to persuade the donor to give. Although the receipt of the gift will be deferred until after the donor's death, its size is likely to be more substantial than a lifetime donation. There is a tendency to believe that legacies are for the big national charities and for smaller and local charities to ignore this source of income. But the evidence is that this is not so, that if the smaller charities can remind their supporters that making a bequest is a good way of helping the charity, then they too will be able to take advantage of this important tax relief.

If a charity is a residual beneficiary of an estate, when the legacy is paid over by the executors, it will consist not only of the capital sum, but also of the accrued interest and dividends received by the estate. Where these have been received after deduction of tax, the charity will be able to reclaim the tax paid from the Inland Revenue in the normal way. And it is important to remember to put in a claim as soon as the taxed income is received.

3. Loan-covenants

If a donor makes a capital gift, the money is paid out of his assets, and the only tax advantage is any saving in Capital Transfer Tax which would become due on death if the money had not been given to charity beforehand. If a donor makes a gift out of income under

Deed of Covenant, then the charity is able to reclaim Income Tax at the basic rate, and the donor, if he pays higher rate tax, is eligible for Higher Rate Relief.

It is possible to extend the advantages of a covenant to single gifts by an ingenious device known as a loan-covenant or deposited covenant. The method involves the donor lending the money interest-free to the charity, and then the repayments of the loan by the charity to the donor are offset by payments made by the donor to the charity under Deed of Covenant. For example, if a donor wished to give £1,000 to a charity, by entering into a loan-covenant scheme, he would:

(a) Loan the charity £1,000 repayable in four equal annual instalments, the first such repayment being made the day following the commencement of the loan;

(b) Enter into a Deed of Covenant for £250 per annum (net) for four years, the covenant payments to coincide with the due dates for repaying the loan;

(c) Undertake to waive the loan on death. This is to avoid problems with a deceased's estate, and the normal wording of a Deed of Covenant also states that the covenant agreement will terminate on the donor's death if this occurs before the covenant has expired.

The charity will receive the £1,000 immediately and will be able to reclaim the Income Tax on the covenant payments as they are made; the charity will reclaim £107 Income Tax in each of the four years making the total value of the donation equal to £1,428.

This may seem to be a complicated procedure, but once the charity has a set of printed forms designed for the purpose, it is really quite easy to get them filled in. There need in fact be no actual exchange of payments as the loan is repaid by the covenanted payment, except that separate accounts need to be kept in the charity's books. The donor will have to sign a Certificate of Deducation of Tax (each year, if the annual net covenant payment is over £130).

By this device the charity receives a 42.8 per cent increase in the donation. The donor is also eligible for higher rate relief (up to the maximum level permitted in any year) on the covenant payments as they are made each year, thereby reducing the cost of the donation to him if he is a higher rate taxpayer.

INDIVIDUAL GIVING

There are two problems. Firstly a covenant payment to be eligible for tax advantage should be a payment out of income and has to be accepted as such by the Inland Revenue. *Section 53* of the *1970 Taxes Act* covers covenant payments not out of income and obliges the donor to deduct Income Tax at the basic rate in respect of the covenant payment and pay this tax to the Inland Revenue. So if a donor wishes to give £100,000, there would be little point in making the payment under Deed of Covenant, as it would be unreasonable, if not impossible, for the donor to make payments out of income amounting to £25,000 per annum (or even £10,000 per annum if the period of the covenant were extended to 10 years). The test will be what is reasonable, but except for very large donations there will not be any problem on this count in getting the donor to give in this way.

Secondly there can be problems if the donor dies during the period of the transaction. These problems are to do with Capital Transfer Tax and relate to the amount of the loan outstanding at the time of the donor's death when repayment is waived. This amount will be aggregated with the other gifts made to charity and be subject to the £250,000 limit. It should be noted though that the annual payment made during the twelve months period before death is an income payment and will not be included in the total of capital transfers in the year preceding death and upon death. Most loan-covenants are not large enough to cause any real concern, but very occasionally there may be instances where a charity will need to take some precautionary action.

The *1980 Finance Act*, by reducing the covenant period and introducing Higher Rate Relief, has made loan-covenants a far more attractive proposition. Not only does the charity receive the tax benefits stemming from the donation much sooner, but the cost of the donation to a high rate taxpayer is much reduced. For example for a donor who pays tax at the highest rate of 75 per cent, the effective cost of a £1,000 donation under a loan-covenant arrangement would be reduced to £357 after Higher Rate Relief; and the charity would receive a total of £1428 from the donation and the basic rate Income Tax it can recover. If possible any donor wishing to give a reasonably substantial sum to charity should be persuaded to give in this way, as it is very much to the advantage of the charity, and it will also benefit the donor if he is paying higher rate tax.

49

Gifts in kind

Gifts in kind made to a charity are exempt from Capital Gains Tax. The transfer of an asset to a charity by a donor is treated as a disposal on which neither a gain nor a loss is made, regardless of the original purchase price of the asset and its value at the time of transfer. This exemption applies both for outright gifts and for sales of an asset at not more than cost, whatever the current market value of the asset. In addition under *Section 145* of the *1979 Capital Gains Tax Act*, a charity is exempted from paying Capital Gains Tax on any chargeable gains arising from any sale of assets that it owns, provided that the gain accrues to the charity and that the resulting funds are applied for charitable purposes only.

There are several ways in which the tax situation can be used to the mutual advantage of donor and recipient:

(a) Where a chargeable asset is to be donated to a charity for use by the charity, there will be no Capital Gains Tax liability for the donor; however, if the value of the asset at the date of transfer is LESS than the original purchase price, then it would be to the advantage of the donor to sell the asset to the charity at its market value, and at the same time donate the purchase price to the charity. This will allow the donor to establish a capital loss. And if the purchase price is to be donated, this should be done under a loan-covenant agreement where possible, in order to achieve the maximum tax advantage. It should be noted that Capital Gains Tax is only payable in respect of sales of certain types of assets. It does not extend to wasting assets (such as motor cars), but it would be chargeable on a house which is not the donor's main place of residence or on investment assets to be donated to the charity.

(b) If the purchase price is to be donated under a loan-covenant agreement, then it would still be advantageous for the donor to sell the asset to the charity and donate the purchase price, where a capital gain is being shown. Any liability to Capital Gains Tax would be more than offset by the tax advantages of the loan-covenant. The charity would purchase the asset from the donor at its market value, and the donor would donate the net proceeds of the sale after deducting any Capital Gains Tax liability.

(c) Where the charity intends to realise an asset which it is to receive as a donation, and if the asset is showing a loss on its original purchase price, it would be far better for the donor to sell the asset separately and to donate the proceeds of the sale (again under a loan-covenant arrangement where possible). Note that this would only apply in respect of assets on which a capital loss could be established. Where no capital loss could be established, then it would still be more advantageous for the donor to sell the asset if the proceeds were then donated under a loan-covenant agreement.

(d) Where the charity intends to realise the asset and a taxable gain is being shown, by donating the asset to the charity the donor would save any Capital Gains Tax liability. But by selling the asset separately and donating the net proceeds of the sale after paying Capital Gains Tax under a loan-covenant arrangement the tax advantages will be somewhat greater, although the benefits will not be received immediately.

(e) Where a donor intends to donate a sum of money to a charity and also during the same year to sell an asset on which a chargeable gain will accrue, it would be more advantageous to donate the asset to the charity, which could then sell it free of Capital Gains Tax. However, this would not be as advantageous as making the gift under a Deed of Covenant or a loan-covenant arrangement.

The *1982 Finance Act* made radical changes to Capital Gains Tax, and the impact of these changes will be felt progressively more over the years. The effect will be that many transactions will become no longer liable to Capital Gains Tax, and where there is a liability it will be much reduced. The main changes made were to raise the threshold up to £5,000 annually, and to index-link the cost price of the asset so that its value is adjusted for any inflation after it has been held for one year.

Collecting from the public

Research shows that most people only give to charity when asked. This seems logical and is supported by the old adage *'If you do not ask, you will not get'*. For most charities looking for money, the key is to find suitable people to ask, and then to approach them in a way that is likely to be successful. The problem very often is that charities do not exploit all the opportunities that exist for raising money from the public.

In fact anyone can solicit money for any cause, so long as it is legal and provided that it is not being done under false pretences. People can raise money for political activity, to finance an invention or an invasion, or to get a novel published, or indeed for anything they can persuade people to support. There are only two circumstances where fund-raising is regulated in order to protect the public. These are where collections are made in public rather than through a private approach. The first is for street collections, and the second is for house-to-house collections. In both these cases permits are needed and a stringent set of regulations has to be adhered to.

1. Flag days and other street collections

The regulations cover the collection of money for the benefit of charitable or other purposes. They also cover the sale of articles otherwise than 'when the articles are sold in the ordinary course of trade and for the purpose of earning a livelihood and no representation is made by or on behalf of the seller that any part of the proceeds of sale will be devoted to any charitable purpose'.

Mostly charities use street collection permits for collecting money from the public, giving the donor an emblem, a sticker or a flag in return for the donation. It should be noted that the supply of emblems to the public is free of VAT except when they are sold for a specified sum. There is also the potential for using street collections to sell small items. There may be some possibilities here for raising money, but it does give the potential supporter an additional reason to refuse – they don't like the item AND they don't wish to support the charity.

Street collections come under *Section 5* of the *1916 Police, Factories etc. (Miscellaneous Provisions) Act*. In pursuance of this Act, the Home Secretary has issued a set of regulations governing the conduct of street collections. There is a slightly different set of regulations for the London Metropolitan Police Area than for elsewhere.

Collections will only be allowed with a permit. The local licencing authority (to whom requests for permission to hold a street collection should be addressed) is the local District Council where the collection is to be held or, in London, the Metropolitan Police. There is no system of national licencing, although those national charities which collect nation-wide apply for and get permits to collect in each area where they plan to have collectors on the street. Permits must be obtained in advance. In the London Metropolitan area permission must be obtained on or before the first day of the month preceding the month in which the collection is to be held. Elsewhere the period is usually one month in advance. This is the minimum period and charities are well advised to plan much further ahead than this.

The granting of permits is at the sole discretion of the licencing authority. Some of the criteria that may be used are:

(a) Has the proposed date been booked by another charity? For example, many of the larger charities such as Christian Aid, the Royal British Legion, Geranium Day, Alexandra Rose Day, etc. have particular dates set aside each year and these dates are booked from year to year. It is important for a charity hoping to run a flag day to see what dates are booked and what dates might be available, and to book a suitable date at an early stage in their planning.

(b) Is the organisation a registered charity? Although in theory collections can be made 'for the benefit of charitable or other purposes', most licencing authorities will only grant permission to collections made for charities.

(c) Is it appropriate that the charity undertakes the collection in the way proposed? In Birmingham, for example, groups are only permitted to collect in the centre of the City if they have previously organised a successful collection in another part of the City. In the Metropolitan Police area certain dates are set aside for local collections confined to a borough or part of a borough when groups intending to collect in a restricted part rather than the whole of the London area can apply; applications for local collections must be accompanied by a letter of sponsorship from the Mayor of the Borough concerned. Each licencing authority will have its own policies for the charities it will allow to hold street collections in its area, and for where these street collections can be held.

There are strict regulations on the manner in which the money may be collected, how it is handled after collection and the reporting of the outcome of the collection. Charities wishing to run a collection should refer to the Regulations which can be obtained from the Licencing Authority. The main conditions required are:

(a) A chief promoter and two other representatives of the charity shall be responsible for the collection.

(b) No collection shall be made except upon the day and between the hours stated in the permit.

(c) A collection may be limited to certain districts, streets or public places at the discretion of the Licencing Authority.

(d) Each collector must have a written authority signed on behalf of the chief promoter and shall produce that authority on request to do so. No person under 16 may be a collector in the London Metropolitan area. Promoters may be authorised to allow collectors aged 14 to 16 if accompanied by an adult. Collectors are normally restricted to paved areas, except when a collection is permitted in connection with a procession when collectors may be permitted to collect on the roadway.

(e) Collectors should not cause danger, obstruction, inconvenience or annoyance to any person; a collector should not importune any person; a collector should not be accompanied by an animal.

(f) Collectors should remain stationary; collectors, singly or in pairs, should be at least 25 metres from another collector. (This does not apply in connection with a procession.)

(g) Every collector must carry a collecting box which should be securely closed and sealed and numbered consecutively. The collecting box should prominently display the name of the charity. All money received by a collector should immediately be placed in this collecting box.

(h) Collecting boxes should be delivered unopened to a promoter and opened in the presence of a promoter and another person or by an official of the bank if it is delivered unopened to a bank.

(i) No payment by way of reward shall be made to any collector. No payment shall be made to anyone else connected with the promotion or conduct of the collection except where approved by the Licencing Authority.

(j) Within a stated period (3 months in London) a statement of the outcome of the collection shall be provided in the required form and certified by one or two of the promoters and an accountant (as required).

Street collections include all collections made in public places (except collections taken at open-air meetings), and include for example collections made in connection with carol singing in the street. Collections on private property are not regulated although they must be conducted with the permission of the owner of the premises. And in these circumstances none of the restrictions mentioned above would apply. It is not generally realised how extensive the opportunities for collecting on private premises are, as such premises include:

Cinemas and theatres;

Many shopping centres and malls (which are often owned by the local authority or a property company);

Railway and underground stations (which are owned by the relevant transport authority);

Steps of churches and other areas within the curtilage of buildings.

Collections may also be made without a licence at open-air meetings, although a permit will be required to hold such meetings. In order to organise a street collection the charity needs to be able to get the support of sufficient collectors to make the exercise worthwhile. It is for this reason that national collections are undertaken by national charities. Although smaller charities can obtain a permit to collect within a more restricted area it is also possible for them to combine to hold a city-wide or a country-wide collection; Alexandra Rose Day and the London Joint Annual Flag Day are instances of this.

The Alexandra Rose Day is a good example of a nationally organised collection to help local organisations. Any organisation which cares for the aged, the sick, the disabled or the young may apply to participate. Collecting boxes and flags are supplied together with all the documentation required for a street collection. The local group is allocated an area and is then responsible for finding collectors and collecting as much as it can. It will then receive back in the form of a donation approximately 80 per cent of the amount that its collectors have collected. The balance covers the administrative costs of the scheme. Anyone wishing to organise a collection for Alexandra Rose Day should apply to the Organising Secretary, 1 Castelnau, Barnes, London SW13 9RP.

To give an example of the diversity of charities that take to the streets the following organisations planned to hold street collections in London in 1982 (not including local collections):

Age Concern
Age Concern Greater London
Alexandra Rose Day
British Epilepsy Association
British Leprosy Relief Foundation
British Polio Fellowship
British Red Cross Society
British Rheumatism and Arthritis
Children's Day
Christian Aid
Church Army
Cruse
Geranium Day
Greenpeace
Guide Dogs for the Blind Association
Help the Aged
Imperial Cancer Research Fund
King George's Fund for Sailors
Lest we forget
Leukaemia Research Association
London Federation of Boys Clubs

London Joint Animal Flag Day
Mencap
Mental Health Foundation
Mind
Multiple Sclerosis Society
National Schizophrenia Fellowship
National Society for Cancer Relief
Oxfam
Royal Air Force Association
Royal British Legion
Royal National Lifeboat Institution
St David's Home
St John Ambulance Brigade
Sea Cadet Corps
Spastics Society
United Nations Association
Variety Artistes Ladies and Children's Fund
Voluntary Service Overseas
World Wildlife Fund

2. House to house collections

House-to-house collections are governed by the *1939 House to House Collections Act* and the *1947 House to House Collections Regulations*. As for street collections this licences the collection of money or sale of goods for the benefit of a charitable purpose. Under the 1939 Act, 'charitable purpose' means any charitable, benevolent or philanthropic purpose, whether or not the purpose is charitable within the meaning of any rule of law; 'collection' means an appeal to the public made by means of visits from house to house (including places of business) to give, whether for consideration or not, money or other property. A licence is required, and the licencing authorities are the same as for street collections. The licence authorises collections from house to house, or shop to shop, or pub to pub (with the owner's consent).

There are two exemptions:

(a) 'Where the Secretary of State is satisfied that a person pursues a charitable purpose throughout the whole of England or a substantial part thereof and is desirous of promoting collections for that purpose . . . an order may be issued exempting that person from applying for a licence for making collections for that charitable purpose in areas described in the order.'

(b) If the collection is for a local charity and is for a period of less than 14 days in a local area, the Licencing Authority may issue a Certificate of Exemption of a Local Collection of a Transitory Nature. This releases collectors from some of the more stringent requirements of the regulations.

Unlike a street collection, permission for which is given at the discretion of the Licencing Authority (and which may be withheld for any reason), charities have a right to undertake house-to-house collections, and a licence may only be withheld on certain specified grounds. The following are the grounds for refusal:

(a) That the total amount to be applied to charitable purposes is inadequate in relation to the proceeds. Commission fund-raising, which is a highly successful method of raising money in the USA, is generally frowned upon in Britain. In this country people mostly believe that fund-raising has or should have no expenses attached, and a promoter has to show a reasonably low level of expense before a licence will be granted;

(b) That any one person is to be remunerated disproportionately in relation to the proceeds;

(c) That the granting of a licence would facilitate the committing of an offence under the Vagrancy Act;

(d) That an applicant is not a fit and proper person (the applicant is the promoter of the collection, not the individual collectors) or has not exercised due diligence in the past in running a collection;

(e) That the applicant has not furnished or refuses to furnish proper information in connection with the application.

If an application is refused, the applicant may make an appeal to the Home Secretary.

Application for a licence or for an exemption should be made on or before the first day of the month preceding the month in which the collection is to be held. Applications must be made to all the local licencing authorities where the collection is to be held. Licences normally cover any period up to 12 months.

As with street collections there are a strict set of regulations covering a house-to-house collection. The main provisions are:

(a) Each collection must be run by a promoter who should be a 'fit and proper person'. All collectors must have a Certificate of Authority and a badge bearing their own signature. This must be in a prescribed form, and can be purchased from HM Stationery Office on production of the relevant part of a licence to collect.

(b) Collection must be by way of either a securely sealed collecting box or envelopes with gummed flaps (or both). Collectors with envelopes will often deliver these in advance with an accompanying letter asking for a donation and stating when they will call.

(c) Collectors should be at least 16 years old (18 in London).

(d) Collectors should not importune any person to cause annoyance or remain in the doorway of a house if asked to leave.

(e) Collectors must return collecting boxes and envelopes on request from the promoter or at the end of the collection or if the collector ceases to be a collector.

(f) The handling of the proceeds shall be undertaken in a prescribed manner which is similar to that for street collections.

House-to-house collections can be an extremely effective way of raising money for a charity which commands a measure of national support and has available local groups and volunteers who are prepared to put in the legwork, or for local charities collecting in their local area. It does require effective organising and a commitment from supporters, but the amount raised does increase directly in line with the amount of effort put in.

The most successful door-to-door selling is done by encyclopaedia firms which employ a highly trained salesforce using a well worked out sales patter to sell an expensive product which one would readily believe that most people would not want. There is a clear lesson here for charities. Although they are not selling a product but a 'cause' or a solution to a social problem, the situation is similar. They are approaching an audience predisposed NOT to give and they have a limited time to get their message across. They have first got to spark the interest of the prospective donor and make him disposed to listen; and then they have to sell the cause and get as large a donation as possible. A belief in the cause by the collector is obviously important, but a well worked out approach and some training can increase the chances of success immeasurably.

Collecting boxes

Collecting boxes may be placed on private property with the permission of the occupier of the property. No special licence is required. Collecting boxes placed outside shops will usually be within the boundaries of the property (rather than on the street, where they would not be permitted except under the conditions for street collections).

Collecting boxes normally take one of two forms: firstly a sculpted model made of plastic put outside a shop, and secondly a small box or other receptacle placed on a counter. The yield from collecting boxes is not enormous, but it will increase in direct proportion with the number of boxes placed.

Most boxes are essentially passive collecting devices. Except for outdoor sculpted boxes which seem particularly attractive to young children, there is little incentive for people to give other than goodwill or the fact that they have small change in their hand. One area which charities might usefully explore is the design of collecting boxes. The use of micro-electronic devices or action-sculptures where something (pleasurable) happens when a coin is inserted could transform fund-raising through collecting boxes. It is only the same principle which make space invaders and other amusement machines so successful at persuading people to part with their money.

4. Grants and donations

When an organisation is seeking a grant from central or local government, a grant-making trust or a company, the question often arises as to whether the recipient organisation is required to be registered as a charity before it is able to obtain a grant. For a grant-making trust which is itself a charity, the project or purpose for which the money is being sought has to be charitable. The same also applies to company donations if the donations are to be paid via a Deed of Covenant and be an allowable expense in calculating the company's tax liability. Beyond this, in most circumstances the donor will often insist that the recipient organisation has charitable status as a matter of its own donations policy rather than for any legal requirement.

To this extent there are considerable benefits in an organisation having charitable status, and the problem only arises for those organisations which have not yet obtained charitable status or which cannot or do not wish to do so. Provided the activity for which the donation is being sought is charitable and falls within the terms of reference of the grant-making body, it is often possible to come to some arrangement for paying the donation via a third-party charity. A grant for the general expenses of the non-charity or for any aspect of its work which is not charitable would not be allowed. And the third-party charity paying over the grant would have to supply to the Inland Revenue a statement of the purpose for which the grant was made. If this is done, then there should be no difficulties.

The other main problem in relation to grants and donations is whether they are liable for VAT. The basic situation is that unless the donation is a payment for a service which is of benefit to the donor it will not be liable to VAT. If it is such a payment, then it will be considered not a donation but the supply of a service; and to the extent that the supply is a taxable supply, the payment received by the charity will be taxable if the charity is registered or obliged to register for VAT.

61

Government grants

In this section we will look at the restrictions on local authority grant-making to charities and other non-profit organisations. Much the same considerations will also apply in respect of grants made by central government departments and by quasi-autonomous non-governmental organisations (QUANGOs).

When government talks about the non-governmental sector, whether it be in the arts, education or social welfare fields, it normally refers to 'voluntary organisations' and 'the voluntary sector'. On the whole it tends not to distinguish between those non-profit organisations that are constituted as charities and those organisations which are not. To give one example, the *1977 Housing (Homeless Persons) Act* specifically empowers the Department of the Environment and local authorities to make grants to voluntary organisations in the field of homelessness. The organisation applying would have to prove that it could make an effective contribution to the problem of homelessness but would not have to show that it was charitable in the strict legal sense in order to be eligible for a grant.

There are two instances where charities are specifically mentioned in the area of local authority grant-making:

(a) The *1974 Housing Act (Sections 13, 29–32)* states that only those housing associations and societies which are charitable are eligible to receive Housing Association Grant. So any organisation wishing to use Housing Corporation or Local Authority money to build subsidised fair rent housing needs to be registered with the Housing Corporation and constituted in the prescribed way.

(b) *Section 137* of the *1972 Local Government Act* empowers local authorities to offer public support to a wide range of organisations for activities that are 'in the interests of their area or any part of it or all or some of its inhabitants' and which are not permitted under any other powers at their disposal. To effect this they are allowed to support 'any charitable body in furtherance of its work' or 'any body which provides any public service . . . otherwise than for the purpose of gain'. So although charities are specifically mentioned, charitable status is not a requirement as there is also the power to support other benevolent non-profit organisations. It is a requirement that the organisation supported with a grant under *Section 137* should be a 'non-profit organisation'. In theory the local authority is empowered to support any charity, be it Eton College, the British Goat Society or the Lord's Day Observance Society, if it believes this to be in the interests of some of the inhabitants of the area; in practice what is supported will depend on what the local authority itself believes to be of real interest to the well-being of the local community.

In general, therefore, a non-charity should be equally eligible to receive local authority support as a charity, providing that it is operating for the benefit of the area and that is established not-for-profit. However, local authority grants committees (or those committees which are responsible for deciding which organisations should receive grant aid) may set out certain conditions over and above the legal requirements of what they are empowered to do for the organisations they are prepared to support. These conditions could, and often do, include that the organisation be a registered charity and that its annual accounts are audited. The first of these criteria would be based on the fact that the local authority might believe that a charity had been screened as being a worthy organisation, and that this offers some sort of protection against anything going wrong. But the test of charitable status is what the organisation is empowered to do in its objects and not its ability to carry out its activities. However, by restricting its grant-making in this way, it does provide a convenient excuse if anything goes wrong. The local authority could then say: 'Oh well, it was a registered charity and we could not have foreseen that the trustees would run off with the money!' A requirement that the books be audited would seem to make more sense as this does provide a check on how the money is being spent.

A voluntary organisation wishing to obtain a grant from its local authority should first seek to find out whether there are any requirements for eligibility; and if there are, it will either have to reckon with these or attempt to get its grant processed as a special case.

The status of the recipient organisation may be important when applying for a grant. But when the local authority contracts out services which it would otherwise have to perform itself (be it housing maintenance, the provision of overnight accommodation for homeless families, cleaning the streets or running a sports centre) it is able to use commercial companies as contractors, as well as non-profit organisations. The protection here is the contract to perform a specific service for a stated sum, whereas with grant-making the link between payment made and service provided for the benefit of the local community is much more woolly (although it might figure prominently in the application for grant aid, when the organisation will try to show what a suitable recipient it is and how cost-effective it is in what it does).

Grants from trusts

Almost all grant-making trusts are established as registered charities under UK law. As a consequence they enjoy tax relief on their endowment income and on any capital gains they make. In return for this very substantial tax advantage they are obliged to restrict their activities within their charitable objects and they are only able to spend their money for charitable purposes. One of three situations can arise:

(a) The trust objects state specifically that the trust can only give money to registered charities. Any non-charity would therefore be unable to receive a grant from this type of trust quite simply because it is not in the trustees' power to make such a grant.

(b) The trust objects state that the trust may give for charitable purposes, but the trustees have decided as a matter of policy that they will only give to registered charities. Once this policy is decided the trust is as restricted as for the previous category. This sort of policy is common. It is a convenience for the trustees as they do not want to be having to decide what is a charitable purpose and what is not; the Charity Commission and the Inland Revenue will have already done this for them. They also will not have to explain or justify their grants as being for charitable purposes when putting in their claim to the Inland Revenue for tax exemption.

(c) The trust objects state that the trust can give for any charitable purpose or for particular charitable purposes, and the trustees are able to make grants to charitable organisations as well as to non-charities and to individuals with the proviso that the money is spent for charitable purposes. Some trusts have been established specifically to provide grants and bursaries to individuals for educational purposes or to make payments to individual deserving cases for the relief of poverty and these would also fall within this category.

The first point to note is that only charitable work can be supported by grant-making trusts. There are two important exceptions to this. The first is that certain trusts which make grants in the UK may be based abroad and fall under the tax laws of another country. What they can and cannot do may then be slightly different from a UK-based trust. The most notable example is the 'Gulkenkian Foundation', which is based in Lisbon and established under Portuguese law. The other category is the non-charitable trust which does not choose to register as a charity and, as a consequence, is not able to enjoy the tax advantages of a charity. This type of trust pays tax on its income and on its capital gains, and it is allowed to make grants to whomsoever it pleases, including to non-charitable organisations and for non-charitable purposes. There are only two such trusts active in Britain in the field of social change. Both are offshoots of larger charitable empires established by Quaker chocolate manufacturers. There is the 'Joseph Rowntree Social Service Trust', which has close affinities with the Liberal party and has funded a whole spectrum of political and social causes. The sort of work it supports can be illustrated by the way it provided money for John Tyme, a prominent anti-motorway campaigner, so that he could provide help and expertise to local groups fighting motorway public enquiries; this was a campaigning non-charitable activity which was believed to be of community benefit. And there is a much smaller Cadbury trust which mostly provides money for projects in the Birmingham area. So the non-charitable trust is a rarity, although for certain types of non-charitable activity it has provided a lifeline.

The second point is that most grant-making trusts fall into the first two categories and make grants only to organisations that are registered as charities. An organisation which is not registered as a charity is much less likely to get a grant from a trust, simply because few trusts will be able as a result of their constitution or policies to support it.

There is a way round for organisations that are not charities and that either do not wish to or cannot within their present structure register as charities, and also for those organisations which are intending to register as charities but have not yet obtained charitable status. This is that the grant-making trust is requested to pay the grant to a third party organisation with the condition that the grant be paid by that organisation to the non-charity applicant. This intermediate organisation will have to be a registered charity. It will also have to have the power to make grants for charitable work. And the work of the applicant organisation will have to fit in with its charitable objects. If these three criteria are met, then there is unlikely to be any problem. To give some examples of how this might work:

A grant for an ethnic minority project might be routed through the local Community Relations Council.

A grant for a local writers group might be routed through the Regional Arts Association.

A non-charitable organisation wishing to get a grant from a trust should first discuss the mechanics of how the grant is to be paid with the trust at an early stage to see whether the trust can make the grant directly or, if not, whether the payment through a third party is acceptable. Secondly, the organisation will have to find an intermediary charity prepared to act in this role which has objects and activities which do not rule out giving for the purpose for which the applicant requires the grant.

Company donations

A payment made by a company to a charity will not be regarded as a proper business expense and will not, therefore, be allowable against tax. There are two exceptions to this:

(a) **Sponsorship and joint promotions:** If the payment can be justified as a proper business expense for example as part of its public relations, staff relations or marketing expenditure, as is the case with most business sponsorships and joint promotion activities, then it will be an allowable expense for tax purposes. This is dealt with more fully in the section on Sponsorship.

(b) **Annual payments under Deed of Covenant:** If the payment is an annual payment under Deed of Covenant then it will be an allowable deduction against the total profits of the company as reduced by any other relief from tax, other than Group Relief, under *Section 248(3)(a)* of the *1970 Taxes Act.* However, the company will have to pay Income Tax in respect of the covenant payment made to the charity, although this Income Tax will subsequently be recovered by the charity.

Corporation Tax is presently at 52 per cent. Thus to have £100 after tax to pay to charity, a company would have to earn £208.33 before tax, assuming that it was paying Corporation Tax at the full rate and that the payment was not allowable against tax. There is also a small company rate of Corporation Tax of 40 per cent for those companies earning less than £90,000 per annum, and in this case the company would have to earn £166.67 before tax in order to be able to pay £100 to a charity after tax. For companies whose profits are between £90,000 and £225,000, there is some reduction in Corporation Tax liability according to a complicated formula set out in *Section 95* of the *1972 Finance Act,* and a company with profits in this range will pay Corporation Tax at a rate between the reduced rate of 40 per cent and the full rate of 52 per cent; the cost before tax of making a payment to charity will be calculated accordingly.

The financial advantage for a company to give to charity in a tax-effective way is very considerable. A large company can increase the size of its donation by over 108 per cent and a smaller company by over 66 per cent at no extra cost to itself, either by arranging that the payment is by way of a sponsorship or joint promotion, or by paying the money as a donation under Deed of Covenant. If the money is paid to charity in one of these ways, it will be allowable against tax, and the company would only have to earn £100 before tax in order to make a £100 payment to charity.

It should be noted that the charity itself derives no additional benefit from a company covenant, except that because it saves the company money, it might lead to companies increasing their level of giving. The company decides on the size of the donation it wishes to make and then, using a 'gross' covenant form, it pays the amount less Income Tax at the basic rate to the charity, and at the same time it pays the Income Tax to the Inland Revenue, and this Income Tax is later reclaimed by the charity. For example, if the company wishes to give £1,000 it pays £700 to the charity and £300 to the Inland Revenue, and after reclaiming tax the charity will have received £1,000. The main problem with a Deed of Covenant is that it requires that payments are made for at least four years. Like individuals, companies do not like to be tied down to supporting a particular charity over a number of years. So many have arranged their charitable giving to take advantage of the tax situation, whilst at the same time giving themselves the maximum flexibility in determining which organisation to support. The main tax-effective ways in which companies give to charity are:

(a) The company takes out a covenant in favour of a particular charity. This may happen for capital appeals where the company wishes to give a large donation or where the cause is something that the company is predisposed to support on a continuing basis.

(b) The founder or proprietor of the company sets up a charitable trust which is endowed with capital assets transferred by him and operates independently but alongside the company. This trust is a grant-making trust operating in a similar way to other grant-making trusts. However, it exists so that the charitable donations which the company (or its Directors) wishes to make are channeled through the trust.

(c) The company sets up a charitable trust which is funded by covenants made by the company to the trust out of its trading income. The company gets the full tax benefit of making its charitable donations under Deed of Covenant and the trust is able to make one-off donations to the charitable activities it wishes to support. Such a trust, if it is not in occupation of premises and if it has income from investments or other property not exceeding £15 a year, is excused registration with the Charity Commission as a 'small charity'.

(d) The company uses the facility of the Charities Aid Foundation (or some other similar scheme) which acts in effect as an intermediary or half-way house charity in the same way as the company-funded trust (*see* (*c*) *above*). The company makes a covenant to the Charities Aid Foundation, which then reclaims the Income Tax and makes charitable donations to charities at the direction of the company. With the Charities Aid Foundation scheme the recipient of the donation must be a registered charity.

The required status of the recipient to be eligible for a grant is similar to that for trust giving. Where the money is given by a direct covenant (*Method* (*a*)) or via the Charities Aid Foundation (*Method* (*d*)) the recipient must be a registered charity; where the money is given in some other way, the situation will depend on the precise terms of the trust deed, or the policies of the trustees. In most circumstances only registered charities will be supported.

Most large companies have organised their charitable donations to take advantage of the available tax benefits. However, some smaller companies have not and are not aware of the benefits of making donations under covenant. Particularly when approaching smaller companies at a local level, a charity should seek to find out whether the company intends to make the donation under covenant. If it does not, then the charity can:

(a) Try to get the company to make out a covenant in favour of the recipient charity. A covenant of half the intended donation over four years would yield the charity double the originally intended donation at a lower overall cost to the company (where the company is paying Corporation Tax at the full rate).

(b) Draw the company's attention to the services of the Charities Aid Foundation (48 Pembury Road, Tonbridge, Kent TN9 2JD) and hope that the goodwill that accrues as a result will lead to a larger donation or continuing support for the charity.

With smaller companies the tax advantages are likely to be smaller as the company will probably be paying the lower rate of Corporation Tax (assuming that it is making a profit!). However, the advantage is still considerable – more than half as much again as the tax advantage available to individual donors making donations under Deed of Covenant.

There is another potential problem; the company might be a 'Close Company' with a restricted range of shareholders. In this case the charitable donations made by the company may be apportioned by the Inland Revenue amongst the shareholders for tax purposes according to the size of their shareholding in the company. This could mean a higher rate tax liability for the shareholders, although since the *1980 Finance Act* which introduced Higher Rate Relief, this apportionment of the company's donations would have to bring any shareholder's total gross covenant payments to charity over the £3,000 level before it had any affect on the shareholder. This is a situation which seldom arises, but it is a factor that should be borne in mind for donations from close companies where the shareholders and the company are both giving substantial sums to charity under Deed of Covenant.

VAT and the receipt of grants and donations

In general, donations received by charities and voluntary organisations are not deemed to be the proceeds of a business activity and are therefore outside the scope of VAT. This also means that any VAT paid on the costs incurred in the fund-raising cannot be treated as 'input tax'. So the VAT paid by the charity on telephone charges, consultancy fees, printing of covenant forms, etc. in respect of its fund raising cannot be offset against the charity's 'output tax' or reclaimed from Customs and Excise. Where any goods or services purchased by the charity are partly for its fund raising and partly for business purposes (in respect of a chargeable or zero-rated supply) then an apportionment of the VAT that has been paid will be made and only that part which relates to the business supplies will be able to be treated as input tax.

Where a charity receives a grant which is to be used either to provide a specific benefit to a particular person or for a specific purpose of benefit to the donor, the grant is to be treated as a payment for a business supply which the charity undertakes to provide, and not a donation to aid the charity's good works. If the CBI, for example, gave a grant to an arts research organisation to undertake a survey of industrial sponsorship of the arts then this would probably be deemed to be of benefit to the organisation making the grant, and therefore a business supply. Where there is no benefit to the donor and the grant is not earmarked to provide a specific benefit to a particular person, then no VAT will be chargeable.

It is the current fashion to talk about 'value for money' in the services that charities provide and to show how this compares with the cost of providing similar services in other ways. This inevitably leads to the idea of 'contracting': that the charity provides a specific service for a stated sum which is paid by a government or local government authority. This would then not be treated as a grant but as a business service. In return for 'X thousand pounds' or 'Y pounds per head' the charity will provide recreational facilities on a particular piece of open space or overnight accommodation for homeless persons or whatever. All these will be business supplies and liable to VAT.

The liability to charge VAT will only exist where the total of the charity's supplies brings it above the VAT exemption limit. So there will be two circumstances in which charities will need to take this into account:

(a) Where the 'grant' is deemed a payment for a service and this brings the total value of goods and services provided by the charity over the exemption limit obliging the charity to register for VAT; the acceptance of the grant in these circumstances will raise other issues that the charity will have to take into consideration.

(b) Where the charity is already registered for VAT or is obliged to register for VAT as a result of the payment; if the grant is to be a payment for a service this should be clearly discussed at the outset, and it should be agreed whether the grant to be paid is inclusive or exclusive of VAT. The difference to the charity is considerable:

Inclusive grant	£10,000
VAT	£1,300
Net available to the charity	**£8,700**
Gross amount paid by donor	**£10,000**

71

GRANTS AND DONATIONS

Exclusive grant	£10,000
VAT in addition	£1,500
Net available to the charity	**£10,000**
Gross amount paid by donor	**£11,500**

Much will depend on the way in which the conditions attached to the grant are worded. If they are worded so tightly that the payment is brought within the VAT system, then if the amount of the grant is an exclusive amount and VAT is added to the total paid to the charity, then this will actually benefit the charity as it will be able to offset any input tax paid on goods or services it purchases in the course of spending the grant. If on the other hand the charity receives a pure grant where no VAT is chargeable, it cannot offset this input tax; this will in effect mean that it will have to spend rather more to provide the same service. For some donors (e.g. government and local government) it will not matter whether VAT is added or not; and so it may in fact be beneficial for the charity to think in terms of providing a contracted service, provided that the amount it is applying for is agreed as the VAT exclusive figure.

5. Company giving

In the Section on Grants and donations we showed that a donation to charity in order to be allowable against tax must be made under Deed of Covenant. Usually the company will organise its giving through a charitable trust or via the Charities Aid Foundation in order to take advantage of the tax concessions without being committed to support a particular charity for four (or more) years. There is no tax advantage to the charity, but the tax advantage to the company is as shown below:

Corporation Tax rate	Tax advantage
0%	0%
40%	+66.7%
52%	+108.33%

Where a company pays no Corporation Tax there is no advantage in organising its donations to charity under Deed of Covenant. Where a company does give under Deed of Covenant, this provides a ceiling to the donations it makes — if it exceeded this, any additional donations would cost the company more than double the amount given away, unless further Deeds of Covenant were taken out. Because most company giving is undertaken under Deed of Covenant, it provides a measure of stability to the amount given by companies to charity. In a bad year the company will still have outstanding commitments to pay (except when it undertakes to covenant a proportion of its profits to charity); so the fact that the company is doing badly will not necessarily mean that its donations programme has had to be severely curtailed.

Sponsorship

There is a growing trend for companies, particularly the larger companies, to try to get some 'return' for the money they spend on donations. This return will range from a brief acknowledgement, through to a full-scale identification of the company with the project supported via a sponsorship deal.

In certain circumstances where the term 'sponsorship' is used loosely to describe what is in effect only a publicised donation, the 'sponsorship' payments can then be made under the company's donations programme which will be organised under Deed of Covenant in order to obtain the full tax advantage. It should be remembered that a donor (and this includes a company donor) paying under Deed of Covenant should receive 'no appreciable benefit' in return for the donation.

There will also be other limited circumstances when the benefits received are not substantial and payments might still be made under covenant. For example, corporate membership schemes, perhaps giving preferential booking arrangements or facilities for corporate entertainment, might be cases in point. This again could only be described as 'sponsorship' when using the term in its loosest sense.

A sponsorship payment will normally be treated in the same way as any other business expense, for it is a payment for a marketing or promotional service supplied to the company. As a business expense it will be a deductible expense for tax purposes provided two conditions are met:

(a) The payment must be of a revenue nature. It cannot be a capital payment.

(b) The payment must be incurred wholly and exclusively for the purposes of the trade of the company.

Under the first of these conditions it will be seen that sponsorship of a building or of building works will not be an allowable expense, even if the building is named after the sponsor and the sponsorship generates substantial publicity. This does not mean that a company cannot sponsor a capital project; it simply means that its sponsorship payments will not be treated as a business expense for tax purposes and will have to be paid out of the company's after-tax income. In the case cited, however, a company could make a series of annual payments as a donation under Deed of Covenant for the same purpose, as it is not a true sponsorship; and in this way it would retain the tax advantage, because the benefit would not normally be seen as substantial in relation to the size of the payment; and in any case whatever benefit there is would be largely incidental to the purpose of the payment, the provision of the building. Similarly any payments made for fixtures and fittings, equipment, the purchase of works of art, and other similar expenditures would not be deductible expenses even if the second condition were met.

The second of the two conditions means that sponsorship payment must be made (and justified) as a payment solely for a business purpose. Thus there should be no element of philanthropy in the payment, although the fact that the payment (for the purposes of the trade of the company) may be made to a registered charity and be applied for the benefit of that charity is not relevant in this context.

Although the position stated here represents the basis on which the Inland Revenue assess the eligibility of any payment as being deductible, the company has only to be able to justify the payments as being made solely for the purposes of the trade. The motives for undertaking the sponsorship and the fact that the company may in fact be spending the money partly for philanthropic purposes will not matter, if it can justify the return it is getting as a reasonable return for its expenditure. In practice, so long as the payments are small in relation to the turnover of the company and the expenditure results in a reasonable amount of advertising or publicity or PR for the company, then the Inland Revenue will not normally raise any objections. However if the payment is clearly not in furtherance of the trade of the company then it will be disallowed as a business expense.

It should be noted that the cost to the company for an allowable covenant payment and the cost to the company for an allowable sponsorship payment are identical. But it is one of the ironies of charitable giving that the letter of the law dictates that a payment must be made either for no return (as a donation under covenant) or for a full return (as a sponsorship) for it to be a deductible expense. However a great deal of company support for charity normally falls somewhere between these two extremes; for a donation the company might require an acknowledgement and be happy with some publicity for what it is doing, and for a sponsorship it might not be able to justify it as the most cost-effective way of furthering its trade (indeed many businessmen are on record as saying that they would not be able to fully justify sponsorship purely in business terms). The Inland Revenue are reasonably flexible in that they do allow a certain amount of benefit in return for a covenanted donation and they do not examine in any great depth whether a sponsorship is wholly and exclusively for the purposes of the trade. It is on the whole something of a 'grey area'; putting one's name to a building may be philanthropy, whereas putting one's name to a concert may be sponsorship, but in either case a company needs to understand the tax situation if it is not to fall foul of the Inland Revenue. Equally a charity seeking financial support from a company should understand the situation so it can frame its application accordingly; and when seeking sponsorship it will naturally want to stress the benefits that the company will receive in return for its money.

There is a slightly different situation regarding VAT. If the payment to the charity is a true donation no VAT will be chargeable. If it is a payment for a service then VAT will be chargeable (if the charity is registered for VAT). A true donation is a payment made freely by a donor who decides its timing and amount. The donor may give a general direction as to how the money should be applied, but will not receive ANY supply of goods or services in return for the donation or as a consequence of it, whether or not the services supplied are substantial in relation to the payment made. Customs and Excise accept an acknowledgement of the donation and even some measure of publicity for it as reasonable; and this by itself would not turn a donation into a taxable supply. However if free refreshments are made available to the sponsor, or if free advertising space is given in a brochure, then the payment would be deemed to be in respect of a taxable supply.

The criteria that Customs and Excise use are different from that which the Inland Revenue use. If a charity is registered for VAT it should discuss the VAT situation with the sponsor beforehand. And for most companies it will make little difference whether VAT is chargeable or not, as they will be able to offset this against their own output tax. If acceptance of the sponsorship would oblige the charity to register for VAT, it may in some instances be worth the charity devising a scheme which is not taxable, and checking this out with Customs and Excise beforehand.

Gifts in kind

Gifts in kind are a useful source of help for charities that companies can make at little cost to themselves. Companies, for example, can donate to charities materials that are surplus to their present needs or which are no longer required. This might cover end of lines from their stock-in-trade, waste materials, old office equipment which is being replaced, or even an out-of-date (for them) computer. A company may also donate materials or stock-in-trade of some value to such things as raffles or tombolas or for whatever purposes the charity can prise these things out of the company.

There are two aspects of the tax situation. The first is whether VAT will be charged to the company by Customs and Excise in respect of the cost of the donation; and the second is whether the cost of the donation will be an allowable expense against the company's profits for Corporation Tax purposes.

With regard to VAT, the company will be liable to pay VAT on the cost of the item (at cost or written down value whichever is the lower) if it is a taxable supply. If, for example, a department store donates a teddy bear to a charity for a raffle, and the book value of the teddy bear is £5, the company will be liable to pay 75p in respect of the donated teddy bear. It is the normal practice for a company to donate items which have been wholly written off in their books or, where possible, to write off the value of the item before donating it. This is not always possible and where it cannot be done the company (not the charity) may be liable to VAT. If the charity is purchasing the item at cost, below cost, or at a substantial discount, then the tax situation is similar, but the charity will also have to pay VAT on the purchase price at which it buys the item.

Whether or not the gift is allowable as a deduction in computing Corporation Tax liability is determined by *Section 54* of the *1980 Finance Act*. *Section 54* provides that *Section 411(8)* of the *1970 Taxes Act* (which disallows the cost of certain gifts) shall not preclude the deduction of expenditure incurred on a gift to a charity, but the expenditure must still satisfy *Section 130(a)* of the *1970 Taxes Act* as being wholly and exclusively for the purpose of the trade. So the general provision is that gifts to charity made for the purposes of the trade of the donor company are an allowable expense, and gifts that are made not for the purposes of the trade are not allowable.

Section 54 replaced *Extra-Statutory Concession B7* which allowed certain small gifts to local bodies established for education, cultural, religious, recreational or benevolent purposes. Any such gifts to local bodies which are not charities (and which do not come under *Section 54*) will still be allowable under *Extra-Statutory Concession B7*. To qualify for relief any expenditure on such a gift must be incurred wholly and exclusively for the purposes of the trade of the company, it has to be small in relation to the donor's business and it is only available for gifts to *local* bodies.

Advertisements in charity brochures

One way in which charities often seek money from companies is through advertising in charity brochures, annual reports, etc. The advertising can seldom be justified as anything except philanthropy.

The company may pay for the advertising out of its charity budget using income it has paid under Deed of Covenant for the purpose of making charitable donations. The Inland Revenue permit a reasonable level of publicity in return for a donation, and this method of paying for charity advertising should cause no problems. The company may also treat the expenditure as advertising expenditure incurred in the course of its trade, when it would be an allowable expense in calculating its Corporation Tax liability. Provided the company can justify the expense as a reasonable business expense, there will be no difficulty. Whichever way the payment is treated, the tax situation will be the same. Some large companies will have a specific budget for paying for advertising space in charity brochures as part of their support for charities.

The VAT situation is slightly more complicated. Under *Group 5* of the *Zero Rate Schedule*, the publication of an advertisement in any newspaper, journal or periodical is zero-rated. The preparation of such an advertisement or the supply of services in securing such an advertisement (eg. design, agency fees) are also zero-rated. One new form of charity fund-raising involves taking a page of a national newspaper and getting companies to pay to have their names included in the advertisement. This would fall into the *Group 5* zero-rating.

Where the advertisement is in a publication which is issued annually or less frequently it will not be eligible for zero-rating and VAT will be chargeable at the full rate. However, there is a concession for advertisements in charity brochures, annual reports, etc., where the advertising is considered to be a donation and therefore outside the scope of VAT. Four conditions laid down by Customs and Excise have to be met if this is to happen:

(a) The brochure should be published by a charity and have the characteristics of a charitable fund-raising exercise;

(b) The payment made for the advertisement is clearly excessive by normal commercial standards in relation to the space taken and the circulation of the publication;

(c) The motivation of the advertiser is to support the charity; and

(d) The brochure includes a significant proportion of non-business advertising paid for by private individuals. Private advertisements are regarded as those which say, for example, *'Good wishes from (or 'space donated by') John and Susan Smith'*, but not those with otherwise similar wording taken out by, say, *'John and Susan Smith, Grocers, 49 High Street, Newtown'*.

Where a charity is registered for VAT (or would be obliged to register for VAT if the advertising in its brochures were standard-rated), then this is a valuable concession. Charities should note particularly the fourth condition, and make a positive attempt to secure advertising from their individual supporters. Advertising in any pamphlets or books produced by the organisation would be excluded from this concession under the first condition, and would therefore be liable to VAT if the charity is registered for VAT.

6. Membership subscriptions

Many charities have members and income from their membership subscriptions is an important source of funds for their work. There are two important tax aspects of subscription income, which it is important to be aware of when designing a subscription scheme. The first is the liability of subscriptions to VAT. VAT will be chargeable on subscriptions except in certain circumstances. Under *Groups 6* and *9* of the *Exempt Schedule* certain subscriptions are exempted. There is also a concession for 'charitable' associations whereby if no benefit is received by the member other than an annual report and voting rights, the subscription is treated as a donation and is outside the scope of VAT. Where the member does receive benefit as a result of the subscription and part of the benefit is in the form of goods or services which themselves are exempt from VAT or zero-rated, then VAT will be chargeable on only a part of the subscription income.

The other tax advantage is that where the member receives no appreciable benefit, the subscriptions may be paid under Deed of Covenant if the organisation is a registered charity. This allows the charity to recover Income Tax at the basic rate (currently 30 per cent) on the amount of the subscription, (thereby increasing its value by 42.8 per cent) and the donor to claim higher rate relief (if he pays tax at a higher rate and has not used up his full entitlement to the relief).

The combination of these two tax benefits is of considerable importance. The extra value of a covenanted membership subscription to the charity is 42.8 per cent less any additional administrative expenses that are incurred by having the subscription paid under Deed of Covenant. If a membership subscription incurred the maximum liability to VAT, it would reduce the income received by the organisation from its subscriptions by fractionally over 13 per cent. It is important therefore that an organisation get the terms and conditions of its membership subscription scheme right. There is the potential to increase the amount of money actually received by nearly two-thirds, firstly by avoiding liability to VAT and secondly by introducing a covenant scheme and encouraging members to pay their subscriptions under Deed of Covenant. Where membership income is substantial or where this is seen by the charity as an area of fund-raising that could be developed, the benefits of reducing any liability to VAT together with the benefits of being able to reclaim income tax on subscriptions paid under Deed of Covenant could be considerable.

VAT Liability of membership subscriptions

In general, the provision by any club, association or society or facilities or advantages to its members in return for an annual subscription or other consideration is deemed to be a business activity. And such subscription income is liable to VAT, if the organisation is obliged to be registered for VAT (the exemption limit is £17,000 of annual taxable turnover in 1982–83). VAT at its current rate of 15 per cent will be payable at a rate of 13.04 per cent on the total (gross) subscription income received.

However, for charities there are a number of situations where the organisation will be wholly or partially relieved of having to pay VAT on its subscription income. The rules are quite clear, and any organisation intending to introduce a membership subscription scheme should study them carefully, firstly to determine whether there will be any liability to VAT and secondly to see whether any small amendments to the terms of membership would enable the VAT liability to be reduced.

There are two situations where subscriptions are exempt from VAT:

(a) **Youth club subscriptions:** A youth club is regarded as a non-profit organisation whose rules restrict membership to young people below the age of 20 which provides a programme of cultural and recreational activities suitable to the requirements of its members. The annual membership subscription paid by members which entitles members to benefit from the facilities provided by the club is exempt from VAT. Any additional payments made directly for other similar activities (eg. for trips, holidays, particular sporting activities) are also exempt. That part of the subscription which represents an affiliation fee of the youth club member to a regional or national association is also not taxable. The affiliation fee that a youth club itself pays as membership of a regional or national association is also regarded by Customs and Excise as falling within the exemption and are not taxable. The precise details of VAT liability of youth club subscriptions are set out in *Group 6* of the *Exempt Schedule* (Customs and Excise Notice 701).

(b) **Professional bodies and trade unions:** Membership subscriptions to professional bodies and trade unions are exempt from VAT despite the fact that membership brings very real benefits to the members; and the following fall within this exemption:

(i) A trade union or other organisation which undertakes as its main objective the negotiation on behalf of its members of the terms and conditions of employment;

(ii) A professional association where membership is customary if not obligatory for those pursuing a career in the particular profession;

(iii) Learned societies and other associations concerned with the advancement of a particular branch of knowledge, or the fostering of professional expertise, where membership is restricted to those directly connected with the purposes of the association;

(iv) A lobby group which makes representations to the government on legislation and other public matters affecting the business or professional interests of its members where membership is restricted to individuals or companies whose interests are directly connected with the purposes of the association.

The supply of any right of admission to any premises or any conferences, performances or other event to which non-members have to pay to attend is not included in this exemption. Part of an otherwise exempt subscription may be liable to VAT at the standard rate on this account. Where an association wishes to institute an additional charge to non-members to attend events or conferences it should first examine whether the additional revenue that this will generate will more than compensate for any VAT liability that is created.

In addition this exemption is restricted to the package of membership benefits available in return for their subscriptions; it does not include the supply of goods or services which do not relate to the aims of the association as set out in its constitution or those which are paid for separately. The precise details of the treatment of subscriptions to professional associations is given in *Group 9* of the *Exempt Schedule (Customs and Excise Notice 701)*.

For 'charitable' associations which look for support from the general public, the subscription income may in certain circumstances be treated as a donation and entirely outside the scope of the tax. If payment of a membership subscription secures for a member the availability of no personal facility or advantage of any kind other than the right to receive formal reports of the organisation's activities and the right to participate in its management, the subscription income will not be taxable. For an organisation to qualify for this concession, it need not be a registered charity, although it must not supply any benefits or rights to its members other than such things as annual reports and accounts and voting rights at the Annual General Meeting.

This concession where the membership subscription is regarded as being outside the scope of VAT only operates where the member receives no benefit for his subscription. And this is quite strictly interpreted. In many instances a member will receive some tangible benefits. Some of the benefits received may be in the form of exempt or zero-rated supplies on which no tax will be chargeable – this might include professional training undertaken at below cost (exempt) or a monthly bulletin or free copies of the society's publications (zero-rated). In these circumstances the subscription income is 'apportioned' for VAT purposes into a chargeable and non-chargeable part as follows:

MEMBERSHIP SUBSCRIPTIONS

(a) The value of goods and services supplied which are full-rated supplies, which will be chargeable to VAT at the full rate; and

(b) The value of goods and services supplied which are exempt or zero-rated, which will not be liable to VAT.

It should be clearly noted that the criteria which Customs and Excise use to consider whether subscriptions are taxable for VAT purposes bear no relation to whether the Inland Revenue deems the member to be in receipt of any substantial benefit when deciding whether a covenant is valid for tax purposes (*see below*). Thus a covenant scheme for a museum or similar organisation's membership subscriptions might be allowed even when membership brings the right of free or reduced price admission (this is in fact the case with the National Trust), whereas Customs and Excise would hold that the membership subscription is a payment in return for taxable benefit. The Customs and Excise interpretation of whether the member receives any benefit is far more restrictive than that of the Inland Revenue.

Apportionment of membership subscriptions into the taxable and non-taxable parts is normally carried out by the organisation, although Customs and Excise will want to accept the basis on which this is done. The organisation can get Customs and Excise to agree a consistent formula for computing the VAT liability on its membership subscriptions, which will be used from year to year. It can also submit any proposed formula for discussion and agreement before using it. Where the non-taxable parts of the subscriptions are trivial as compared with the taxable parts, no apportionment will be allowed and the whole of the subscription will be liable to VAT.

One common method of apportionment is on the basis of costs. The apportionment would be made on a basis that reflects the cost to the organisation of providing the various benefits supplied to its members. The fact that a particular member (or members in general) do not avail themselves of certain benefits (for example, a members room may be provided which is virtually unused) is of no concern in calculating VAT liability; it is the fact that the benefit is made available which is important. Another possible basis of apportionment is on the basis of value. If, for example, a subscription to a journal costs £6 per annum and membership which gives the member the journal and other taxable benefits costs £8 per annum, the organisation could claim that the subscription element

85

of the membership (which would be zero-rated) would amount to £6, leaving £2 to be apportioned to the other benefits provided. Whether this basis would be acceptable would depend on whether it could be justified by the organisation as being reasonable.

For most 'good cause' charities membership subscription income will either be able to be treated as a donation or the major benefits will be in the form of non-VATable items. By careful wording to the terms and conditions of membership the VAT liability might be considerably reduced or even avoided. For example, if use of a library or clubroom is confined to members then this would be a chargeable benefit; whereas if the same benefits were freely available to members and non-members alike (although non-members were unlikely to hear of them or avail themselves of them) then it could reasonably be claimed that such facilities were not a benefit of membership. For many other types of charity (such as museums, theatres, galleries) membership subscriptions or friends schemes will be sold and taken up on the basis of the benefits that are offered, and in these cases VAT will be chargeable on either the whole of the subscription income or a substantial part of it, and the charity should accept this with good grace and budget for it accordingly.

Covenanted subscriptions

If membership subscriptions are paid under Deed of Covenant, then the charity will be able to reclaim Income Tax at the basic rate on the covenant payments. With a basic rate of Income Tax at 30 per cent, this would increase the amount received by the charity from the subscription by 42.8 per cent on those subscriptions which are paid under Deed of Covenant. In addition, if the member pays tax at a higher rate, then he will be eligible for higher rate relief and the actual cost of the subscription to him will be reduced, and the value of this relief will be dependent on the tax position of the donor, as is shown in the table on next page. This can be an added inducement for getting members to pay their subscriptions in this way.

Whether a covenanted membership subscription is eligible for these tax advantages will depend on what benefits the member receives in return. In theory a covenant should not be a payment for

MEMBERSHIP SUBSCRIPTIONS

Highest tax rate paid	Cost to the member of a £10 covenanted subscription	Value to the charity of a £10 covenanted subscription
30%	£10.00	£14.28
40%	£8.56	£14.28
45%	£7.85	£14.28
50%	£7.14	£14.28
55%	£6.43	£14.28
60%	£5.71	£14.28
65%	£5.00	£14.28
70%	£4.28	£14.28
75%	£3.57	£14.28

goods or services or other benefits. In practice the test is whether the benefits are appreciable or not.

The law is unclear on what will be considered an appreciable benefit, but generally the Inland Revenue adopts a lenient attitude to charity subscriptions. For example, a member of the National Trust is able to receive free entry to all the properties that the public pays to visit and still pay his membership subscription under Deed of Covenant. This is a considerable benefit to the member, and in practice it is probably the main reason for people joining. The National Trust's scheme is allowed by the Inland Revenue. On the other hand the Inland Revenue won a court case some years ago against the Torridge Festival Society and disallowed a scheme where membership brought the right to reduced prices at the festival events.

A charity obviously wants to make its membership scheme as attractive as possible as an inducement to get people to join. The provision of benefit in return for a covenant payment is a 'grey area'. The fact that there are no clear guidelines probably benefits charities, as some of the schemes that have been allowed would probably not have been allowed had the guidelines been more clearly formulated. When considering a scheme a charity should first think of the benefits it can reasonably provide. And before actually introducing the scheme it is well advised to get the approval of the Inland Revenue; otherwise it runs the risk of having its scheme disallowed after having gone to considerable administrative expense to launch it.

Covenanted membership schemes will only provide a tax advantage where the member pays Income Tax at the basic rate or higher. Also they can only be introduced for registered charities (in Scotland and Northern Ireland, for organisations that have been determined to be charitable by the Inland Revenue). For non-charities there will be no tax advantage. For charities in the course of registration the tax advantage will only be obtained when registration is granted, although if the charity can show that it was operating 'for charitable purposes only' prior to registration it will be able to recover tax on any covenant payments it received prior to the actual date of its registration as a charity.

There are two problems associated with covenanted membership subscriptions. The first is that a covenant to charity must be capable of lasting for a period of four years or longer, if there is to be any tax advantage. And this long-term commitment to the charity may be a deterrent to many members. The National Trust, which has the largest membership of any British charity, has a covenanted membership scheme which lasts 'during my lifetime or until I resign my membership', and this allows the covenant to lapse when the member resigns. This form of wording appears to give the member the power to revoke the covenant agreement unilaterally at any time, which should make the covenant ineffective for tax purposes. However, the wording of the National Trust's deed of covenant has been accepted by the Inland Revenue.

This form of wording of a covenanted membership scheme does appear to get over the problem of long-term commitment should the member become disaffected with the policies of the charity. But any other charity wishing to implement a scheme where the wording of the covenant may be controversial is well advised to discuss the particular form of wording to be used with the Inland Revenue before implementing the scheme.

The second disadvantage is that the member has to covenant to pay a certain sum for the period of the covenant. If this is a fixed sum, then this will not allow for any increase in the subscription level from year to year, and the tax advantages would be partially offset by the fact that the member's subscription would remain static for the duration of the covenant. This would benefit the member and could provide an inducement for the member to enter into a Deed of Covenant. If the rate of inflation is not too high the charity will not lose out either, as the tax benefits of the covenant will more than offset the lower subscription rates that would be payable in future years.

Most charities would not want to commit themselves to a fixed subscription rate for their covenant members. To allow the subscription rate to be raised, the Deed of Covenant could be worded so that the amount payable each year is the level of membership subscription for the time being in force; the disadvantage then is that if the covenant payments are made by Bankers Order (which is the most usual method of payment) then the member will have to notify his bank of the change in the amount to be paid each time the subscription rate is changed. The most satisfactory method of payment from the charity's point of view is by Direct Debit where the member signs a mandate allowing the charity to debit his bank account with the amount of the membership subscription. The charity will normally agree to notify any subscription rate changes in advance and undertake to provide full repayment in the case of dispute.

Any covenant will cost a certain amount to administer. Unless the organisation has a volunteer to handle the recording of covenants and the claiming of Income Tax from the Inland Revenue, then it is probably not cost-effective to introduce a covenant scheme where the annual subscription level is below £5.

Finally it should be realised that not every member will wish to pay their subscriptions under Deed of Covenant. Although the tax advantage to the charity is 42.8 per cent for those subscriptions paid under Deed of Covenant, if only ten per cent of members elect to pay this way, then this will only give the charity a slightly less than 5 per cent increase in its subscription income. The onus is therefore on the charity to devise an attractive scheme and promote the very real tax advantages for members paying their subscriptions in this way.

7. Lotteries, gaming and competitions

This section covers lotteries, gaming activities, pool betting and competitions run by charities and other non-profit associations and clubs as a means of raising money.

Lotteries including raffles, instant lotteries, grand draws, tombolas and other amusements with prizes are run by many organisations to raise money. The provisions of the *1976 Lotteries and Amusements Act* extended the range of lotteries that could be run, and at the time it was hailed as a new opportunity which would help charities substantially. If the results have been less impressive, it is because there are still substantial restrictions on the size of the lottery and the value of the prizes that can be offered. This section looks at the sort of lotteries that it is possible to run and the circumstances under which they can be run. Further information is available in a NCVO booklet (*see below*).

The running of gaming activities including such things as bridge and whist drives, bingo and gaming machines is another important ingredient of much grass roots fund-raising activity. The promotion of these activities is circumscribed by law, and any promoter needs to be fully aware of whether they are required to obtain a licence and what they can and cannot do. There are concessions that relate to small-scale gaming activities carried out by clubs and associations where the proceeds are applied otherwise than for private gain and these are detailed in this section. However, the detailed conditions under which gaming and lotteries can be run are outside the scope of this book, and we would refer readers to the much more comprehensive guide on the subject *'Lotteries and gaming: voluntary organisations and the law'* (*£1.95*), which is produced by the National Council for Voluntary Organisations.

This section also covers the running of competitions. Provided

91

such competitions are skill-based and do not then come within the provisions of *1976 Lotteries and Amusements Act*, then there is no legislation affecting them. Although competitions must involve a degree of skill, simple competitions established for fund-raising purposes in fact will have many of the attributes of a lottery, but without the legal requirements affecting the running of lotteries or the amount that can be given away in prizes or the total amount that can be raised. Competitions are being used increasingly in marketing and sales promotion, and they are an area which charities should seriously examine for fund-raising opportunities (both for large-scale and for grass roots fund-raising).

Useful addresses for further information:

Gaming Board of Great Britain, 168–173 High Holborn, London WC1V 7AD

Gaming Board (Lottery Department), 64–78 Kingsway, London WC2B 6BW

Lotteries Council (*the trade association for lottery promoters*), 13 Dover Street, London W1X 3PA

HM Customs and Excise (*regarding gaming duties*), King's Beam House, Mark Lane, London EC3R 7HE

National Council for Voluntary Organisations (*for their booklet*), 26 Bedford Square, London WC1B 3HV

Lotteries

The law relating to lotteries is contained in the *1976 Lotteries and Amusements Act*, the *1977 Lotteries Regulations* and the *1981 Lotteries Amendment Regulations*. The current monetary limits are set out in the *1981 Lotteries (Variation of Monetary Limits) Order*. The Act does not specifically define the term 'lottery' but it is generally understood as being '. . . a scheme where an entrant pays for a chance to win a prize; the distribution of prizes (which may be in cash or in kind) is made solely by chance. Where any degree of skill is involved (however little), then there is no lottery . . .' But if there is skill involved, it will be a competition with prizes, which will be discussed separately. Payment may be for cash or for 'other valuable considerations'.

From this basic definition it is readily seen that a lottery can include a number of different types of activity:

(a) A raffle or a grand draw where tickets are sold and a draw is held to select the prizewinners;

(b) An instant lottery where the participant buys a ticket and removes a covering to discover whether he has won a prize or not;

(c) A sweepstake which is in essence similar to a raffle where the prizes are the names of horses competing in a race and the distribution of prizes is determined by the order in which the horses complete the race;

(d) A tombola where the participant draws a numbered ticket which may or may not correspond with a numbered ticket attached to a range of prizes which are won when the numbers correspond;

(c) Various amusements with prizes normally held at fetes, etc. where no skill is involved. A typical example might be a 'guess the weight of the cake' competition, although this particular example might in fact be deemed to be a competition of skill which would fall outside the provisions of the Act.

Four different types of lottery are permitted by law. Of these, one relates to local lotteries run by local authorities to raise money. The other three types are all relevant to charities, although they may be run by or for the benefit of any club or society not established as a commercial undertaking for private gain.

1. Private lotteries

In a private lottery the sale of tickets is confined to members of one society and the promoters of the lottery must also be members of that society. The term 'society' includes clubs, associations, institutions, etc., but local branches or affiliated groups are regarded as being separate societies for the purposes of running a private lottery. The definition of society also includes people who work on the same premises (which for example allows office sweepstakes) or people who live on the same premises.

The society must NOT be established for purposes connected with betting or the running of lotteries. There are in fact a number of societies set up to raise money for charity through organising regular lotteries (these are often known as 100 clubs, 200 clubs etc.). Some police authorities take the view that these are established for purposes of running lotteries and should therefore be regarded as being 'Societies' Lotteries' where more stringent conditions of regulation will apply (*see next page*). Anyone wishing to run this sort of fund-raising activity should consult their legal adviser or the registration authority first to see whether it can be done as a Private Lottery.

The whole of the proceeds of a Private Lottery, after deducting printing and stationery expenses, must be devoted to the provision of prizes or applied to the purposes of the society or both. There is no regulation on the proportion that must go as prizes, except in the case of lotteries run for people who live or work in the same premises where the whole of the proceeds after permitted expenses must be distributed as prizes. The lottery may not be advertised except on the premises of the Society. There are a few other restrictions on the way such a lottery may be run.

The main advantage of a private lottery is that it is far less regulated than other forms of lottery. No registration is required with the local registration authority. There is no limit on the size of the lottery or on the price of the individual tickets. Prizes may be in cash or kind. However, and this is the most important point, the lottery must be confined to the members of the society that is running the lottery. So if you have a forum where tickets might be sold such as a large members meeting or your AGM, then a private lottery does offer a much easier approach, and is a fund-raising opportunity that ought to be considered.

2. Small lotteries and amusements with prizes incidental to certain entertainments

The term entertainment used here includes sporting and athletic events, film premieres, dinner dances and balls, fetes, bazaars, jumble sales and other similar events run by voluntary organisations and charities for the purposes of fund-raising. Very often the organisers wish to raise more money over and above the sale of tickets, and this section of the Lotteries Act permits them to do so by organising a small lottery incidental to the entertainment or event.

In order to qualify under this section the lottery must be incidental to the event and not the only or the only substantial inducement for people to attend. The sale of the tickets and the announcement of the winning tickets must take place on the premises where the entertainment takes place. The whole of the proceeds of the lottery and the whole of the proceeds of the entertainment after deducting the expenses of organising the entertainment and the permitted expenses in running the lottery must be devoted to purposes other than private gain. None of the prizes may be in cash, and there is a maximum of £50 which is the permitted expenditure on prizes.

As with a private lottery there is no limit on the size of the lottery nor on the price of the individual tickets; and again no registration of the lottery is required.

In addition to running lotteries the organisers may also instal gaming machines under the same conditions, where no gaming machine licence duty is payable; or they may run bingo without having to pay bingo duty.

3. Societies' lotteries

A society's lottery is the most usual form of fund-raising by lottery. It is not restricted to the members of the society nor to a particular event. However, the regulations are much more demanding and the lottery must be registered with the appropriate local Registration Authority.

A society's lottery may be promoted on behalf of any society which is established otherwise than for private gain or commercial purposes, including charitable organisations and organisations established for sporting, cultural or recreational purposes. The lottery must be registered with the appropriate Registration Authority (the District Council, or the Borough Council in London) where the head office of the Society or branch promoting the lottery is located. If the value of tickets sold exceeds £10,000 then the lottery must also be registered with the Gaming Board.

Registration with the local Registration Authority costs £20 initially, and there are additional fees payable if more than one lottery is to be promoted in any scheme for which registration is being sought. Registration with the local Registration Authority is in fact no more than a formality.

The number of lotteries that may be promoted by the society, the size of the lottery, the value of the prizes are restricted as follows:

(a) Small lotteries

No prize may exceed £2,000 in value (regardless of the price at which it was purchased or indeed whether it was donated), but prizes may be in cash or in kind. The price of the tickets may not exceed 50p, and the total proceeds of the lottery must not exceed £10,000. The total value of the prizes must not exceed 50 per cent of the proceeds, and the expenses of the lottery that can be deducted must not exceed the amount actually incurred or 25 per cent of the proceeds, whichever is the lower figure.

(b) Short-term lotteries

A short-term lottery is one which takes place less than a month after the date of the previous lottery. The maximum value of the tickets sold in a short-term lottery must not exceed £20,000, and the value of any prize must not exceed £2,000. For this and for other lotteries not in the category of small lotteries registration with the Gaming Board is required.

(c) Medium-term lotteries

A medium-term lottery is a lottery which takes place between one and three months after the date of the previous lottery. The maximum value of the tickets sold in a medium-term lottery is £40,000 and of any one prize £3,000.

(d) Any other lottery

If a lottery takes place more than three months following the date of the previous lottery, the maximum value of tickets sold must not exceed £80,000 nor the maximum value of any prize £4,000. This restriction on the value of a prize in any lottery to £4,000 is probably a limiting factor in the growth of lotteries as a large-scale form of fund raising. This maximum prize should be compared with the £1 million jackpot prizes on some football pools and £250,000 top payment for premium bond winners. There are proposals to have the maximum value of lottery prizes raised to perhaps £20,000, but amending legislation will be required before this can happen.

Normally there should be an interval of one week between the date of one lottery and the next. The date of the lottery is the date on which the winners are ascertained. Where prizes are distributed over a period of time, as is the case with an instant lottery, the date of a lottery is deemed to be the last day on which tickets can be sold. Tickets of a lottery should not be sold after the date of the lottery, and they should not be sold more than three months before the date of the previous lottery. By arranging the dates of the lotteries it is holding but still keeping within the letter of the law, a society can in effect hold 13 short-term instant lotteries simultaneously, for example to coincide with an annual appeal.

The number of lotteries promoted on behalf of any one society in any year should not exceed 52. The limit for the amount of tickets sold on behalf of any one society in a year is therefore just over £1 million (52 × £20,000) and assuming the permitted maximum is taken as prizes and as expenses this would leave just over £250,000 to be applied to the society.

It should be noted that where a society wishes to run more than the permitted number of lotteries, it is able to organise itself to do this without much difficulty. A football team might run lotteries on behalf of the 'North Stand Supporters Club' and the 'South Stand Supporters Club', each being deemed to be a separate society in the context of the lotteries regulations. A theatre might run lotteries directly and through its friends group; a national charity might run lotteries through its head office and via its local branches. What is defined as a society includes 'any club, institution, organisation or association of persons, or any separate branch or association of such a society'.

There are very stringent regulations on how societies' lotteries are to be conducted (*1977 Lotteries Regulations* and *1981 Lotteries Amendment Regulations*). The level of expenses that are allowed is restricted, and this includes the administrative and marketing costs of running the lottery, the printing of the tickets and any discounts (normally 10 per cent) offered to retailers who sell the tickets. The expense level is a percentage of the total sales as budgeted. If all the tickets are not sold this might give a higher than permitted expense level, but the society would be able to justify this on the basis that it did not achieve its budgeted sales levels (although it could not get away with this persistently). Every lottery has a named person as 'promoter', and he is responsible for the conduct of the lottery: the society itself is financially responsible for the outcome of the lottery and not the promoter. Anyone wishing to promote a society's lottery is well advised to read the regulations carefully and fully understand them.

When the *1976 Lotteries and Amusements Act* was introduced it was hailed as a great opportunity for charities to increase their income. Initially there was a great deal of activity and the 'Instant Lottery' which had been legalised in the Act seemed ubiquitous. Things have quietened down somewhat since then. In 1980–81 the Charities Aid Foundation estimated a total lottery income for charities of £11 million or rather less than ½ per cent of the total charitable income received by all charities for the year. This figure was down on the previous year's estimate of £15 million. This figure excludes lottery income raised by local authorities for local projects, which is running at approximately the same level as charity lotteries. Although small, the lottery income of charities is a useful source of funds, and the figures probably considerably understate the amount that is raised through lotteries and raffles by charities and by the many sporting, cultural and educational societies which raise money in this way.

One area that charities have not exploited to the full is harnessing the resources and good will that they can call on into the running of their lotteries. There is certainly scope to run instant lotteries successfully. But there is also scope to devise unusual prizes such as trips and visits and dinners with famous people at little cost to the society, but which may be perceived as being extremely attractive to people buying the tickets. The regulations provide a tight constraint on the running of a lottery, and many charities do find it hard to make any substantial amount of money from lotteries. So some lateral thinking on how they can be run profitably might be helpful.

Competitions

In a lottery prizes are distributed by chance and participants are induced to make a payment in order to obtain a chance of winning a prize. If there is any degree of skill involved there is no lottery. Pool betting requires a participant to make a forecast of a future sporting (or other) event in return for a payment, and prizes are distributed based on the outcome of the event. Gaming is defined as the playing of a game of chance or a game of skill and chance combined for money. Lotteries are regulated by the *1976 Lotteries and Amusements Act*, pool betting by the *1963 Betting Gaming and Lotteries Act* and gaming by the *1968 Gaming Act*.

Somewhere among these three forms of gambling there exists a whole area of competitions where the outcome is decided by the skill of the participant. The legislation affecting competitions is contained in *Section 14* of the *1976 Lotteries and Amusements Act* which makes it unlawful to conduct in or through any newspaper, or in connection with any trade or business or the sale of any article to the public:

(a) Any competition in which prizes are offered for the forecast of the result of either a future event or of a past event where the results are not yet ascertained or generally known (except by bookmakers or pools promoters); or

(b) Any other competition in which success does not depend to a substantial degree on the exercise of skill.

Skill-based competitions are lawful. Whether it is the competition that has to involve a substantial degree of skill, or whether it is the level of skill itself that is required that has to be substantial is not clearly stated in the law. But competitions that involve a mixture of luck and skill are lawful (e.g. match the faces of babies to star personalities AND write a punch line).

Skill competitions are a popular form of sales promotion. They are run, for example, by national newspapers as a regular and popular feature (eg. spot the ball competitions) and they have even been run by individuals wishing to sell their house (this has been an amusing ploy during a period when the housing market has been depressed).

One couple in the North of England tried to raffle their house but fell foul of the law, as their scheme was in effect a lottery, which would be prohibited. The important point is to advise a competition where the outcome depends substantially on the skill of the participants. A couple in Aldeburgh decided to offer their house as a prize in a competition. The competition involved unscrambling 14 anagrams of East Anglian place names (such as 'Laybed', 'Harry Beg' and 'Me bad hen') and then giving a reason for wishing to live in Aldeburgh. The house was estimated to be worth £46,000 and the owners hoped to sell 5,000 entries at £10 each, which would also cover their expenses. Anything raised over and above this was promised to a home for the mentally handicapped, and if they failed to sell more than 4,750 entries they retained the option to declare the competition null and void and return the entry fees. Similarly a 'super match ball contest' was devised to sell a pub in Hitchin, so that its regulars could keep it as a free house. It should be noted that these competitions have often failed to attract sufficient support. In the case of the Aldeburgh house only 3,000 entries had been received by the closing date. One extremely successful competition was the book 'Masquerade', where the prize was a golden hare buried somewhere in England, with the clues given in the book that the competition was designed to promote. This idea had been adapted by the NSPCC as a fund-raising device. They have produced a similar book and buried a gold and silver flute as a prize. In addition, additional clues can be obtained in return for a donation to the charity.

Branch managers, promotion consultants and newspapers are all aware of the popularity of competitions. They have to be devised so that they involve a minimum of skill sufficient to avoid the restrictions of the *1976 Lotteries and Amusements Act*. As a fund-raising device for charities, skill competitions (which are in effect little more than lotteries) are totally underdeveloped and this is an area where many charities might examine the potential. One very real advantage over a lottery is that there are no restrictions either on the size of the take or the value of the prizes that can be offered.

There is another type of competition which relates directly to the purpose of the charity which can be run successfully. A typical example is the National Poetry Competition run annually by the 'Poetry Society'. Participants are required to send an entrance fee with each poem submitted (£1.50 in 1982), and this competition has not only become an important event in the poetry calendar but it is also a major source of funds for the society.

The VAT position on competitions is clear. Competition entrance fees are standard rated and must include 15 per cent VAT if the promoter is registered or obliged to register for VAT. There are two exceptions to this where competition entrance fees are exempt from VAT:

(a) Competitions in sport and physical recreation, where the money paid in entry fees is *wholly* returned in prizes awarded in that competition; or

(b) Competitions in sport and physical recreation organised by a non-profit-making body established for the purposes of sport or physical recreation; but if the organising body includes in the competition entrance fee a charge for the use of its facilities or admission to its premises, then the entrance fee is standard-rated.

For VAT purposes, Customs and Excise define 'Competition' as meaning a structured and organised contest, tournament or race for which a prize or title of some kind is awarded. 'Sport or physical recreation' covers all activities which are generally referred to as sports including such things as darts, snooker, billiards, motor sports, dressage, angling and clay pigeon shooting as well as the athletic sports. However activities like chess, card games, hare coursing, dog and horse showing, model aircraft flying and spot the ball or newspaper competitions are not covered.

If the promoter is a charity and wishes to avoid VAT on competition entrance fees by suggesting that it is in effect a donation to the charity, the liability to VAT will depend on whether it is in fact a voluntary donation and on the wording of the conditions of entry. Charities wishing to do this are advised to discuss the wording first with their local VAT office.

Pool competitions

In general pool betting is regulated by the *1963 Betting Gaming and Lotteries Act*. All promoters must register with the local authority and comply with the requirements of the Act. In addition they must register with Customs and Excise for the purpose of pool betting duty, which is levied at the rate of $42\frac{1}{2}$ per cent (1982–83 rate) on payments made by way of pool betting.

There are two concessions available to charities:

(a) Under the *1971 Pool Competitions Act* promoters of pool competitions for the benefit of charities, sporting organisations or other non-commercial organisations who conducted at least nine pool competitions **in the period 25th November 1969 to 24th November 1970** are granted a licence to continue such operations. The House of Lords had declared that simple pool competitions run by charities were in effect lotteries, and the 1971 Act was passed to enable them to continue running such competitions without having to comply with the more stringent provisions relating to lotteries. It is a transitional measure and the concession relates only to those promoters active in 1969–70 which have continued to run pool competitions.

(b) Under the *1972 Betting and Gaming Duties Act* that part of the payment which is paid to a charity or sporting organisation (whether or not it is paid voluntarily, but provided that the punter knows that the sum is being earmarked for this purpose at the time he makes his bet) is not subject to Pool Betting Duty. Promoters are advised to agree the wording on the coupon with Customs and Excise.

Gaming

Gaming which is defined as playing a game of chance for money or money's worth is regulated by the *1968 Gaming Act*. The main concessions which affect charities are:

(a) *Section 41* of the Act permits small-scale equal-chance gaming at entertainments promoted for purposes other than private gain on unlicenced premises (for gaming purposes) provided that not more than one payment not exceeding £1.50 is made by each player in respect of all games played at the entertainment. The whole of the proceeds after deduction of reasonable expenses and the provision of not more than

LOTTERIES, GAMING AND COMPETITIONS

£150 of prizes (in value not cost) must be applied for purposes other than private gain. This section specifically excludes bankers games and slot machine gaming. It covers most whist drives, bingo sessions, bridge evenings etc. organised to raise money for charity. Where bingo is played under these provisions, no bingo duty is payable.

(b) *Section 40* of the Act provides for the playing of bingo and other equal chance gaming at unregistered clubs with at least 25 members where only small charges are made for the gaming. A maximum daily session charge of £6 for bridge or whist on days when the premises are not used for other forms of gaming or 15p in other circumstances is permitted. These are in addition to any stakes hazarded which must be returned to players in full as cash prizes.

(c) As an alternative to *Section 40*, a members' club (which is a club managed by or on behalf of members and not for purposes of private gain) may register under *Part II* of the Act to provide incidental gaming facilities not primarily for motives of gain and to make charges for doing so for the benefit of club funds. Registration may be refused on the grounds that the club is not a bona fide members' club or that it has less than 25 members or that it has no permanent existence or that the principal purpose of the club is gaming (except for bridge and whist clubs which may register under this section). A registered club has to comply with a set of regulations in its conduct of gaming activities. In addition a registered club is permitted to instal two gaming machines without having to register under *Part III* of the Act. The registration fee is not substantial, £78 initially and £39 on renewal (in 1982).

(d) Gaming machines may be used incidentally at non-commercial entertainments under the same conditions as small lotteries run at such entertainments (*see Lotteries*). Gaming machine licence duty is not payable in such circumstances.

(e) Gaming machines which pay limited prizes for limited stakes (prizes must not exceed £1 in money or £2 in kind and the charge per game must not exceed 10p) can be installed on unlicenced premises on application to the local authority for a permit to do so. Other machines have to be installed under the conditions of *Part III* of the Act. Gaming machine licence duty is payable on all machines (*except see (d) above*) and is chargeable at between £120 and £750 per machine depending on the machine and the circumstances in which it is installed.

(f) Bingo duty is not chargeable on bingo played under *Section 41 (see (a) above)* or on bingo incidental to non-commercial entertainments (*see (d) above*). On other bingo there are exemptions from bingo duty depending on the circumstances in which it is run. The rates of duty and exemptions from paying duty are set out in a notice which can be obtained from Customs and Excise.

8. Investment of charity funds

Under *Section 360* of the *1970 Taxes Act* a charity is exempt from tax on certain income it receives. The following items of investment income fall under this exemption:

(a) Rents, premiums and other profits from land belonging to the charity;

(b) Interest, dividends and other distributions.

The charity may obtain a refund of Income Tax already paid on dividends and interest it receives net of tax by making a claim to the Inland Revenue (Claims Branch). And tax can now also be reclaimed on Building Society interest received net of tax. The exemption only applies if the income is applied for charitable purposes; in effect this means that the income must be spent on the work of the charity or donated for some charitable purpose, or if it is not spent the charity must be able to show the purpose for which the income is being accumulated and that it will eventually be applied for some charitable purpose. If the income is simply accumulated, then the income will be subject to tax, and any tax deducted at source will not be reclaimable.

Under *Section 145* of the *1979 Capital Gains Tax Act* a charity is exempted from paying Capital Gains Tax on any chargeable gains arising from any sale of assets that it owns, provided that the gain accrues to the charity and that the resulting funds are applied for charitable purposes. Whether the reinvestment of the capital gain would be considered an application for charitable purposes is not immediately obvious from reading *Section 145*. However, the Inland Revenue have clarified the situation by stating that for a normal charity the reinvestment of a gain which it had realised

105

would not in itself preclude exemption of the gain by virtue of *Section 145*. So reinvestment is considered an application for a charitable purpose, provided that the investment fund or endowment is itself held for charitable purposes. The gain would not be exempted of course if the proceeds of the sale were applied to some non-charitable purpose, but to do this would be outside the powers of the trustees.

Capital Gains Tax, unlike Income Tax on most forms of investment income, is not deducted at source; and the onus is on the Inland Revenue to collect the tax, rather than on the charity to reclaim it. In practice charities will not have to pay Capital Gains Tax on any gains they make unless they are accumulating money to no purpose. Capital Gains Tax is administered by the Head Office of the Inland Revenue at Somerset House, to whom any queries should be addressed.

A charity is also relieved from paying stamp duty on transfers of assets which have been acquired or donated.

These reliefs are available to registered charities, and also to those charities not required to register (*see Appendix 1*) but which are determined to be charitable by the Inland Revenue. Charities whose registration has not yet been accepted cannot make a claim until they are registered, but they will be able to reclaim tax subsequently (where it is due) in respect of any income and capital gains received prior to registration where tax has been paid; this tax relief will be given on the basis that the organisation was a charity operating for charitable purposes only at that time, although not then registered as such.

There is a possible restriction in the tax exempt status of charities due to the provisions of *Section 22* of the *1973 Finance Act*. *Section 22* provides that in certain circumstances where a shareholder is entitled to tax relief and where the investment represents 10 per cent or more of the particular class of shares outstanding, the tax exemption will not apply. In this case the shareholder will be unable to reclaim tax on the dividend or interest from this investment. The provisions of *Section 22* are of very limited relevance to charities which will only very rarely encounter this loss of tax exemption.

Subject to *Section 22* the three reliefs enjoyed by charities provide a complete freedom from taxation on the investments owned by a charity. This enhances the value of any income a charity derives from its investments, and it provides a greater incentive for a charity to manage its investments and any cash balances it is holding to good effect. The benefits are obviously felt most by those charities that have substantial sums available for investment and least by the small local organisation relying on voluntary income to meet its day-to-day expenses. But even the smallest charity can derive considerable benefit by managing its cash flow as effectively as it can, and then keeping only a small working balance of its funds on current account, with surplus funds placed on deposit or invested. Some of the steps that can be taken include:

(a) Making sure that all grants receivable are received on the due date;

(b) When negotiating grants, ensuring that the grants are received in advance and as early as possible;

(c) Invoicing for amounts due promptly and chasing up unpaid invoices;

(d) Managing the payment of outgoings to the best advantage of the charity.

In making their investments, charities may use the services of the Official Custodian for Charities. This body was created under the *1960 Charities Act* to provide two services: to keep in safe custody charity funds that are transferred to this body; and to remit the gross income from such funds to the charity. The advantages of this service are:

(a) The charity funds are held in safe custody on behalf of the charity;

(b) The administration of the charity's investments is eased, as the paperwork involved in transactions is carried out by the Official Custodian free of charge and the trustees are informed or consulted regarding such things as rights issues or redemptions where action needs to be taken;

(c) There are no problems that arise when a trustee resigns or dies or is simply unavailable in having transfers signed or in respect of the names under which the stock is registered;

(d) The interest and dividends are remitted gross, with the Official Custodian reclaiming any tax that has been deducted at source, which relieves the charity of having to make its own claims.

Further details of the services of the Official Custodian for Charities and of the Charities Official Investment Fund can be obtained from: **The Official Custodian for Charities**, 57–60 Haymarket, London SW1Y 4QZ.

Responsibilities of charity trustees
regarding the investment of charity funds

Charity trustees have a responsibility to protect and manage the property of a charity. The trustees of many smaller charities are perhaps not always aware of this. In a leaflet the *'Responsibilities of Charity Trustees'* the Charity Commission state the following obligations on charity trustees in connection with the management investment income:

'Besides studying the provisions of the governing instruments, the newly appointed trustee should make sure what is the property affected by them and its condition, and who are his co-trustees and others concerned in administering these provisions. Trustees must deal with the property within the limits laid down by the governing instruments. If they are allowed a discretion but are in doubt about the proper exercise of their discretion they should consult the Charity Commissioners, who will be pleased to advise them.

'Trustees must exercise reasonable care in all matters relating to the charity and must always keep in mind the interests of the charity.

'Trustees have the duty of protecting the charity's land, investments and other property. Accordingly, they need to know what condition the property is in, what can be done with it and how it is used or invested. Funds or other property that cannot legally be drawn on for running the charity is its permanent endowment and must be preserved to provide a continuing income. Trustees must see that the permanent endowment is invested to produce a good income while safeguarding the real value of the capital, and that all income due to the charity, including recoverable taxes and rating relief, are received.

INVESTMENT OF CHARITY FUNDS

'Unless the governing instruments make special reference to the trustees' powers of investment, these will be found in the *Trustee Investments Act 1961*. Except in cases where the Act otherwise provides, the trustees may avail themselves of the powers contained in the Act. The Act requires trustees to consider what the needs of the charity are, eg. a high continuing income or a capital sum for use at a future date. The trustees must decide what form of investment will be most suitable for those needs and obtain skilled advice for this purpose; and they must review the charity's investments from time to time. A leaflet (*T.P.1*) explaining the Act and a booklet offering guidance to trustees in selecting and managing the charity's investments are available from the Charity Commission.

'The duties of charity trustees as regards investment may be simplified by contributing charity monies on proper advice to a common investment fund. These funds are established specifically to meet the needs of charities and operate on lines similar to a unit trust, they provide a wide spread of investments combined with specialised investment management which smaller charities individually cannot afford. Trustees should look into the advantages that investment in any of these funds may offer. One such fund, the *Charities Official Investment Fund*, has unlimited powers of investment and all charities may invest in it. Information about the Fund may be obtained from the Charity Commission.'

Permitted investments

In order to obtain the maximum advantage from the tax exemptions on its investment income, a charity should first of all see that cash balances are held on an interest-bearing deposit rather than on current account (except for the small amounts necessary for the smooth running of the financial affairs of the organisation). It is possible to arrange an automatic transfer system to and from deposit account with the bank. For larger amounts the bank can place the money on 7-day deposit on the money market at higher rates of interest. With interest rates at their present relatively high levels, this can amount to a useful and easily obtained source of additional income. Secondly, where there is money invested for the longer term, it is the

109

responsibility of the trustees to see that the money is prudently invested. Because charities are tax-exempt, their investment criteria might be slightly different from the individual tax-paying investor, and this is certainly a factor that should be taken into account in selecting suitable investments.

There are restrictions on how a charity can invest its money and these are set out in the *1961 Trustee Investments Act*. This Act gave trustees the power to invest charity funds more widely than had been possible previously. The Act created three classes of investment:

PART I investments (narrower range):

1. Defence Bonds, National Savings Certificates, National Development Bonds (including Ulster) and British Savings Bonds.

2. Deposits in the National Savings Bank, and Trustee Savings Banks.

PART II investments (narrower range):

1. Fixed-interest securities issued by the British Government (including Northern Ireland), Treasury Bills or Tax Reserve Certificates.

2. Securities guaranteed by the British Government (including Northern Ireland).

3. Fixed-interest securities issued by a public authority or nationalised industry in the United Kingdom.

4. Fixed-interest securities issued and registered in the United Kingdom by the Government of or a public authority in any Commonwealth country.

5. Fixed-interest securities issued and registered in the United Kingdom by the International Bank for Reconstruction, by the European Investment Bank or the European Coal and Steel Community.

6. Debentures issued by a company incorporated in the United Kingdom, with a share capital of not less than £1,000,000 which has paid a dividend on all its share capital in each of the five preceding years.

7. Stock of the Bank of Ireland.

8. Debentures of the Agricultural Mortgage Corporation Ltd. (or its Scottish equivalent).

9. Loans to local authorities and other authorities in the United Kingdom which satisfy certain conditions.

10. Debentures, preference or guaranteed stock of statutory water undertakings.

11. Deposits by way of special investment in a trustee savings bank.

12. Deposits in a designated building society.

13. Mortgages of freehold or leasehold property with an unexpired term of not less than 60 years.

14. Perpetual rent charges on land.

PART III investments (wider range):

1. Any quoted securities issued by a company incorporated in the United Kingdom with a share capital of not less than £1,000,000 which has paid a dividend on all its share capital in each of the five preceding years.

2. Shares in a designated building society.

3. Units in a unit trust authorized by the Department of Trade.

Trustees of a charity may invest in Part I investments at any time as well as hold their funds in their bank account.

In order to invest in Part II investments the trustees must obtain advice in writing, or take advice orally which must be put subsequently in writing, from a person they believe to be competent to give such advice, and they must do this before making the investment, although any written confirmation of oral advice need not be received before the investment is made. This has to be done in order to protect the trustees against any charges of misapplying the funds of the charity. The adviser may be a trustee or an officer or employee of the charity; or he may be an outside person such as a bank manager or stockbroker, etc. Likewise when an investment has been made, the trustees should decide at what intervals it is

INVESTMENT OF CHARITY FUNDS

desirable to review the investment and obtain advice on whether it should be retained or sold, and they should obtain and consider such advice accordingly.

If the trustees wish to make Part III investments, they must first divide their investment fund into two initially equal halves. One half of this fund will be designated for investment only in narrower range (Part I or Part II) investments; the other half may be invested in investments in any of the three categories (narrower range and wider range). Obviously as the market values of the investments in each half fluctuate the total value of each half will become unequal. But the proceeds of sale of any investments in the first half will be restricted to reinvestment in narrower range investments. Any new funds which become available for inclusion in the investment fund must be split equally between the two halves of the fund. The trustees are also bound to take advice on the purchase and retention of Part III investments as is required for Part II investments.

For charities with small amounts to invest which wish to invest in wider range securities, this procedure might be cumbersome and inefficient. Under *Section 22* of the *1960 Charities Act*, the Charity Commission is empowered to establish common investment schemes for charities which are designed to enable charities to pool their capital funds in order to provide more efficient investment (by spreading the risks over a wider portfolio and by obtaining continuous advice and supervision for the fund). A number of such schemes have been established by the Official Custodian for Charities. They are in effect unit trusts for charities. The largest of these schemes is the *Charities Official Investment Fund*, and a charity is able to invest the whole of its available money in this Fund if it so wishes. Other schemes specialise in narrower range investments and the charity can hold the narrower range half of its investment fund in this form.

From the list of permitted investments it can be seen that a charity cannot make an investment in land or in shares of companies incorporated outside the UK or in smaller companies or in companies which have missed paying a dividend in the past five years. However, the charity is permitted to purchase shares in unit trusts or in investment trusts which in turn may have holdings in those sorts of investments. And a charity may hold as an investment shares and property that have been donated to the charity outside the permitted categories for investment.

INVESTMENT OF CHARITY FUNDS

A charity may wish to draw up its own criteria for what it wishes to invest in and what it will not invest in, which may relate to the nature of its work or to the ethical and ideological factors underlying its work. The legal power to do this is contained in *Section 6(1)* of the *1961 Trustee Investments Act*, which states that in the exercise of their powers of investment, the trustees of a charity shall have regard to the need for diversification of investments as is appropriate to the circumstances and to the 'suitability to the charity of investments of the description of investment proposed and of any particular investment proposed of that description'. For example, temperance charities are allowed not to invest in breweries and drink companies, and religious and third world development charities are able to avoid investing in companies active in South Africa.

But the trustees of a charity may wish more generally to exclude certain types of investment on political, social or ethical grounds. The whole subject of investing other than for commercial reasons is something of a 'grey area'. By formulating a policy for what they will or will not invest in beyond the criterion of suitability to the charity as permitted in *Section 6(1)*, the charity trustees appear to be stating that they will make their investment decisions on other than commercial grounds – and this would be in contravention of their duties as trustees and would appear to be inviting action from the Charity Commission.

Whether selling shares in Distillers whilst the claims by thalidomide victims had not been settled by the company as a means of putting pressure on the company (or shares in Turner and Newall because of the incidence of asbestosis amongst the workforce) is permissible or not is not clear cut. In general, the trustees of a charity will be able to base their investment decisions on other than commercial criteria, provided that at the same time they can show that they are exercising their proper responsibilities in the management of the charity's assets.

There are no clear guidelines for charity trustees other than the exercise of common sense and sound judgment, whilst being aware of their duties as trustees to protect the charity's assets and obtain a reasonable return on the investments they make. But the following probably represent the basic ground rules:

(a) There is not likely to be any problem in having a restrictive investment policy, provided that any such policy is not so restrictive that it curtails the trustees' ability to make investments on sound commercial grounds;

(b) Any sale or purchase of a particular asset must be justifiable on commercial grounds;

(c) If a great deal of publicity (and dissent) accompanies the introduction of such an investment policy, then the charity will be more likely to encounter problems.

A similar approach might lead to a charity wishing to use its investment money positively in order to further social change in some way. Whilst it is permissible for the trustees to exclude certain classes of investments or particular investments providing that they are exercising their proper responsibilities, the situation is more complicated should the trustees decide to invest purely in particular classes of investment, such as in local companies or in companies adopting fair employment policies regarding ethnic minorities or whatever. The trustees must take care to show that they are investing the funds prudently and not just for social or political reasons. This does not rule out this form of positive investment but it imposes an additional yardstick that the trustees must use in selecting where to put their money. An example of this approach is Dartington Hall Trust, where there has been a move to reinvest the Trust's endowment in enterprises that promote rural regeneration rather than simply to provide an income (where they felt that, for the most part, many of the companies they had been investing in might have been contributing to continuing rural decline directly or indirectly).

Land

The *1961 Trustee Investments Act* gives no power to trustees for the direct investment in land or property. However, land may be held in the following circumstances:

(a) The charity may receive land or property as a gift or as a part of its permanent endowment;

(b) Land or property may be purchased for use by the charity in pursuit of its charitable objects;

(c) The proceeds of sale of land or property which is part of the permanent endowment may be used for the purchase of other land or property.

No land which forms either part of the permanent endowment (that is property held as capital and subject to a restriction on its being expended as income) or which has been actually occupied for the purposes of the charity may be sold or leased for more than 22 years or otherwise disposed of without the consent of the Charity Commission. Further information on the required procedure is available from the Commission.

The Official Custodian for Charities provides a similar service for the holding of land to the service provided for investments. There are a number of fiscal concessions on land that are available to charities:

(a) Relief on Income Tax and Capital Gains Tax, which is given in the same way as with other forms of investments;

(b) Exemption from Stamp Duty on any conveyance, transfer or lease of land or property to the charity;

(c) Exemption from Development Land Tax on land owned by the charity; under *Section 24* of the *1976 Development Land Tax Act* (as amended by the *1980 Finance Act*) Development Land Tax is not chargeable on any realised development value accruing to a charity on the disposal of an interest in the land. The current rates at which Development Land Tax is chargeable are: for the first £50,000 of realised development value, no tax is payable; and thereafter tax is levied at 60 per cent. There are certain provisions whereby if the charity subsequently ceases to be a charity, tax will become chargeable at that time. The exemption only applies to organisations that are charities. In addition if land which is being used for the charitable purposes of the charity is compulsorily acquired, this will be purchased at a valuation that includes its development value (which is not the case when the land is in other ownership).

9. Charity trading

The first issue relating to charity trading is whether charities are permitted to trade at all. In 1972 the Charity Commissioners stated in their report: 'The raising of money by selling goods . . . is not carrying out a charitable purpose, but exercising a power'. A charity must be established for charitable purposes only and so cannot include amongst its stated aims the carrying out of trade. This does not mean that a charity cannot trade, only that its purpose cannot be to trade. The charity may have a power to undertake trading activities as a means of it fulfilling its stated aims, but such a power must be secondary to its primary aims. Indeed fund-raising in itself is not a charitable purpose, but the means that a charity adopts enabling it to fulfil its charitable objects.

There are two exceptions to this general rule, where the trade is seen as directly furthering the aims of the charity. The first is the sale of goods and services that directly further the charity's objects. A charity is able to sell publications or charge for conferences or for admission to the cultural services it is organising or for the educational services it is providing, provided that these fall within the primary purpose of the organisation. The second exception is where a charity sells goods produced by its beneficiaries. The people producing the goods should be the direct beneficiaries of the charity; any more tenuous link would not be covered by this exception. And the goods should be produced as part of the charitable service being provided. The most typical situation is where a sheltered workshop for the disabled sells the goods produced by the disabled workers in the workshop. In a similar manner a third world development charity can sell goods made by people in the third world projects it supports (although it could not sell third world products generally, on the basis that this created employment and resulted in economic development, as the connection between the beneficiaries and the producers of the goods would be too tenuous).

117

So a charity can have as its objects the promotion of its aims through trade where the trade is directly connected to its aims or directly carried out by its beneficiaries, or it can have a power to undertake trading activities thereby enabling it to further its aims. Both these situations are permitted. But the next question a charity intending to trade has to ask itself is whether the powers contained within its constitution permit it to trade. This is not always the case, and if the organisation does not have the power to undertake trading it cannot then legally do so. It can, of course, seek an amendment to its constitution although this would have to be agreed by the Charity Commission.

Taxation and the profits on trading

Whether any profits arising from the trading will be taxable is the concern of the Inland Revenue. In general the profits from trading are taxable. *Section 360(1)(e)* of the *1970 Taxes Act* provides exemption from tax in respect of the profits of any trade carried out by a charity, if the profits are applied solely to the purpose of the charity and either:

(a) The trade is exercised in the course of the actual carrying out of a primary purpose of the charity; or

(b) The work in connection with the trade is mainly carried out by the beneficiaries of the charity.

Thus in the two instances where trading is permitted under charity law, it is also tax-exempt if the profits are used for charitable purposes. In (b) above, it is permitted that the work is carried out mainly by the beneficiaries and, for example, in a sheltered workshop this enables at least some part of the work to be undertaken by able-bodied people; there are no hard and fast rules as to when the work ceases to be carried out 'mainly' by the beneficiaries, but the main purpose of the workshop should be to provide work for the beneficiaries.

In most instances it is quite clear whether the sale of an item is part of the primary purpose of the charity. For an example, an environmental charity could sell its own publications on environmental issues, but it might find itself challenged by the Inland Revenue if it ran a general environmental bookshop and made a profit on this activity. The sale of promotional items such as T-shirts and button badges is less clear-cut, and here the question of extent may be the critical factor in proving that the trading is exempt under *Section 360*.

There are two further instances in which trading carried out by a charity will not be taxable. The first is in relation to goods donated to the charity for resale, where the Inland Revenue consider the sale of the donated goods as a realisation of a donation and not as trade. So a charity shop selling donated goods would not be taxed on the profit it made. If the same shop were to sell a mixture of donated and bought-in goods it would be exempt only on the profits from the donated goods (except where the shop was run through a trading subsidiary; *see also the Section on Charity Shops*).

The Inland Revenue also have an *Extra-Statutory Concession* (*C5*) which exempts the profits of small-scale trading provided that the following four conditions are met:

(a) The organisation is not trading regularly;

(b) The trading is not in competition with other traders;

(c) The trading is supported by the public because they wish to support the charity (and because they believe that any profits will go towards the charity's work);

(d) The profits arising from the trading are applied for charitable purposes.

This Concession exempts such things as jumble sales, annual bazaars, charity premieres, dinner dances and other similar fundraising activities. It would not cover the running of a coffee bar at a youth club or a school letting out its premises for meetings.

Where there is no exemption, the Inland Revenue has the power to assess the charity to tax on any profits it makes on its trading. A profit has to be made, of course, before any tax can be charged. If there is no profit, there is no tax to be paid. In many instances, the charity may well be able to show that its non-exempt trading is not profitable, particularly when a fair share of the overheads have been allocated to the trading activity.

If the amount of trading undertaken by a charity is so great that it becomes a main function of the charity (in organisational terms) then it may be held that the trading is no longer being undertaken as a power but as a primary activity, and the charitable nature of the organisation will then be destroyed; and as a result the Inland Revenue would then argue that the profits should be subject to tax. What constitutes substantial trade in this context is unclear, and there are no hard and fast rules. One major national charity trades directly to the tune of £3 million annually, but other charities have been advised to consider reorganising their trading at a much lower level. The level at which a charity decides that it has to hive off its trading activities into a separate trading company (*see below*) will depend not just on the attitude of the Inland Revenue, but also on how the charity sees its trading activities developing in the future.

Setting up a trading subsidiary

A charity may be trading in a way that is permitted under its charitable objects and with the profits arising from its trading wholly exempt from tax. In this situation the trading can be undertaken directly by the charity without any problems. A charity may be trading and find that some of its trading profit is taxable. Here the charity will decide what to do based on the extent of its trading and the amount of tax it is having to pay. It may be that the extent of the trading is felt by either the Charity Commission or the Inland Revenue to jeopardise the charitable status of the organisation; and in this circumstance the charity will probably wish to reorganise its trading activity.

The method used which avoids any liability to tax and allows trading to continue without jeopardising the charitable status of the charity is to trade through a subsidiary trading company. The charity establishes a separate limited liability company to carry out the trading, and itself subscribes for the whole of the share capital. To do this the charity needs to have the power to make such an investment in its trust deed. An alternative recommended by the Charity Commission, which is particularly appropriate for smaller charities, is for the trustees or a benefactor personally to subscribe for the share capital and then to donate the shares to the charity. The trading company, which is not a charity and which is organisationally kept completely at arm's length from the parent charity, remits the whole of the profits it makes to the parent charity under Deed of Covenant. Under *Section 248(3)(a)* of the *1970 Taxes Act*, annual covenant payments are an allowable deduction against the trading company's total profits, and in this way any tax liability is removed.

Setting up a trading subsidiary is not difficult, nor need it be expensive. The bill need not be in excess of £300, but it is advisable to use a solicitor experienced in this area of charity law. The device of a trading subsidiary convenanting all its profits to a charity is a tried and tested solution acceptable to the Inland Revenue and favoured by the Charity Commission, who view it as right and proper to separate out the charitable and commercial activities of a charity on a proper legal basis.

There are a number of problem areas that a charity will encounter when organising its trading in this way:

(a) The trading company will not be entitled to rate relief on the property it occupies (except for shops selling mainly donated goods – *see the sections on Charity Shops and Rates*).

(b) Since the trading company is remitting all its profits back to the charity, it will not be retaining any money to finance any expansion or to allow for the impact of inflation. If the company retains any profit for this purpose it will be taxed on this. If it does not, it will need to raise the money in some way. One way of doing this is for the charity to lend money to the trading company at a commercial rate of interest; but to do this it needs the power to do so and to be able to justify the loan as being on a sound commercial basis.

(c) The trading company has to remit all its profits under Deed of Covenant. This needs to be done during the accounting year in which the profit is being made. The trouble is that the company will not know its actual profits until well after the accounting year has ended. What is normally done is that the company makes a provisional payment to the charity based on an assessment of its profitability, and an adjustment is made at some later stage when the true profit position is known.

None of these poses insuperable problems; but where a charity can trade directly without prejudicing its charitable status and with minimal or no tax liability, it is well advised to do so. Some charities embark on a trading subsidiary unnecessarily, either because they do not understand the legal situation or because they are afraid of it. But when a charity is planning to develop and expand its trading it is usually best to set up the proper structure sooner rather than later.

Trading through local branches and VAT

The exemption limit for registration for VAT purposes is a turnover of £17,000 per annum of taxable supplies made by the organisation. Taxable supplies includes supplies of goods and services which are full-rated and also those goods and services which are zero-rated. (For example, the sale of publications and sales of donated items by certain charities are zero-rated and the total of these sales would be included in the total taxable supplies.)

Below the exemption limit an organisation is not required to register, and it will only be allowed to if it can give good reason why it should. Above this figure it is obliged to register (although in certain circumstances an exemption from registration can be granted).

If an organisation is registered for VAT or would be obliged to register as a result of undertaking some trading activity, it can organise itself so that the trading is carried out by a branch of the charity or an association or individual acting on behalf of the charity. Where the trading consists of the sale of full-rated supplies, then no VAT would be chargeable if the branch or association (or association or individual acting on behalf of the charity) had a turnover below the exemption limit of £17,000 **provided that full legal and financial responsibility for the trading is accepted by the branch**. Where the parent charity retains these responsibilities, then the turnover will be deemed to be a part of its own turnover.

So a charity can trade through its branches (and this will be particularly useful for charity shops which do not get the zero-rated concession on donated goods, or which are selling bought-in goods) and not charge VAT (although it would still have to pay a price that included VAT on the items it purchased for resale). Two conditions would have to be met:

(a) The branch retains full legal and financial responsibility; and

(b) The taxable turnover of the branch does not exceed the exemption limit, currently £17,000 per annum of taxable supplies.

10. Charity Shops

There are three quite separate aspects of tax relief for charity shops:

(a) A charity established primarily for the relief of distress or the benefit of animals is zero-rated for VAT on the sale of donated goods under *Group 16* of the *Zero Rate Schedule*;

(b) A charity shop run for the benefit of charity selling mainly (more than 50 per cent) donated goods is entitled to mandatory rate relief and to apply to its local authority for discretionary relief under the *1976 Rating (Charity Shops) Act*.

(c) Profits arising from the sale of donated goods (which are considered to be donations income) or profits arising from occasional small-scale trading (under an Inland Revenue Extra-Statutory Concession) or profits arising from the sale of goods produced by the beneficiaries of the charity or by the charity directly operating within its primary purposes (under *Section 360(1)(e)* of the *1970 Taxes Act*) are not liable to tax.

The criteria for the reliefs under these three headings are quite different and are explained in detail in this section.

Charity Shops and VAT

The supply by a charity established primarily **for the relief of distress or for the protection or benefit of animals** of any goods which have been donated for sale is zero-rated for VAT purposes under *Group 16* of the *Zero Rate Schedule*. This concession exists not just for goods sold in charity shops, but also for sales through fetes, bazaars and jumble sales. The eligibility for this VAT concession depends both on what is being sold and on who is selling it. With regard to what is being sold, the zero-rating is subject to several provisos:

(a) The goods will only be zero-rated if the organisation running the shop is registered for VAT. If it is not registered no VAT will be payable in any case. In order to be registered, the total sales of taxable supplies made by the charity must exceed the VAT exemption limit. For example, a small organisation with publications sales of £4,000 per annum and two charity shops with a total annual turnover of £12,000 would not be obliged to register, since the level of sales would be less than the £17,000 level required for registration (1982–83 figure). An organisation with sales below the £17,000 level can apply for voluntary registration for VAT; and if its sales consist wholly or mainly of zero-rated supplies then it may well be to its advantage to do so. Customs and Excise do not automatically accept applications for voluntary registration, but would normally give an application by a charity sympathetic consideration.

(b) The goods have to be donated. If they are sold to the charity (even at a highly advantageous price), the zero-rating does not apply.

(c) If the charity sells a mixture of new and donated goods, the donated goods will be zero-rated, and the new goods will be chargeable as if they were sold by a normal trader.

(d) If the charity shop sells the goods on commission for the owner, as is the case with some 'Nearly New' shops, then provided the ownership of the stock at no time is transferred to the charity, VAT is only chargeable on the commission charged by the shop, and not on the whole purchase price; but in these circumstances the zero-rating concession does not apply.

(e) The zero-rating only applies to the sale of the goods when sold by the charity. If the goods are subsequently resold by the purchaser, then they will cease to be zero-rated.

126

CHARITY SHOPS

This VAT concession only applies to goods sold by certain types of charities; the eligible categories are as follows:

(a) Charities established primarily for the relief of poverty. If the objects clause of its Trust Deed it is stated that the charity is established specifically for the relief of poverty, it will qualify for the zero-rating. If it is established for more general purposes, but through its policies and programme of activities it is primarily undertaking relief of poverty work, it will still qualify.

(b) Charities established primarily to make provision for the care, relief, prevention or care of people suffering from any disease or disability and for the care of women before, during or after childbirth.

(c) Charities that are established for the protection or benefit of animals.

Although a strict reading of the *Zero Rate Schedule* would indicate that this relief is only available for the sale of donated goods by charities, in practice it is also available when the goods are sold via a separate (non-charitable) trading company, which is owned and operated by the charity or for the benefit of the charity. A letter from HM Customs and Excise to the Charity Trading Advisory Group dated 2nd April 1981 clarifies this point: 'Trading companies may benefit under *Item 1* of *Group 16* if they are themselves charities of the kind set out therein. They may be so regarded if they pay over all their profits to a charity qualifying for relief under *Item 1*'.

What is acceptable as relief of distress and what constitutes other forms of charitable activity is a matter for discussion with Customs and Excise. In most circumstances the matter is quite clear cut. A charity shop operated by a settlement or social action centre would normally be considered as falling within the zero-rating concession, whereas one run by a museum would not. And there will be border-line cases where the charity will have to seek to justify its eligibility for the concession. In passing it should be noted that any charity which benefits animals is eligible, whereas in the case of human animals the situation is much more restrictive.

The zero-rating has two benefits. Firstly it means that the charity is not obliged to charge VAT on its sales of donated items. And secondly, at the same time it can offset or reclaim all of its VAT input tax on goods and services it purchases in the course of running the shop. It should be noted that the turnover of sales of donated goods is included in the turnover of taxable supplies in computing whether the charity is obliged to register for VAT. Thus a charity selling £12,000 donated goods and £5,000 new goods each year through its charity shops would be obliged to register (as per the 1982–83 exemption limit), and VAT would then have to be charged on the sales of new goods.

Where the running of charity shops (or the sale of goods through fetes, bazaars, jumble sales, etc.) brings the total turnover of taxable supplies that the charity is making over the exemption limit, the charity might think of reorganising its sales activities so that its shops are run by individuals or associations or local branches or separate fund-raising charities on their own account for the benefit of the charity. Provided that the total turnover (including donated goods) of taxable supplies made by any one shop or group of shops does not exceed the £17,000 exemption limit, no VAT will be payable. Provided that the individual or association or local branch or separate charity which is organising the charity shop(s) (or fetes, bazaars, jumble sales, etc.) accepts full legal and financial responsibility for its operations, and provided that sales do not exceed the exemption limit, then no VAT will be payable. Persons intending to reorganise their trading activities to avoid paying VAT in this way are advised to discuss how they intend to do it with Customs and Excise to see that the way they are constituted accords with Customs and Excise criteria for being treated separately from the central charity.

The financial benefits of separating off the charity shop into a separate organisation are the greatest for those charities which cannot take advantage of the *Group 16* zero-rating. If for example a countryside preservation charity operated three charity shops each with a total turnover of £7,000 in donated goods, then it would be liable to VAT of £2,750 on its turnover of £21,000. It would save this amount entirely (less any VAT it has paid out on purchases it has made during the year) by organising its charity shops into separate units for VAT purposes. This saving would be well worth the administrative bother.

For a charity which is able to enjoy the zero-rating of donated goods the advantages are far less. For example if a charity has three shops each with a turnover of £5,000 in donated goods, and £2,000 in bought-in goods which are being sold at a 50 per cent profit margin, then the total VAT saving of organising the shops into separate non-VATable units will be £780 less £390 VAT input tax paid on the purchased stock less any VAT paid on its operating expenses — and this will result in only a trivial saving which would not be compensated for by the additional administration that would be required.

Rates and Charity Shops

There are two circumstances where a charity shop will be allowed rate relief:

(a) Where the shop is operated wholly or mainly for charitable purposes. This would include shops mainly selling the charity's own publications and the products it produces in pursuit of its charitable objects. It would also include the sale of products made by the beneficiaries of the charity (in sheltered workshops for example).

(b) Under the *1976 Rating (Charity Shops) Act* a shop which sells mainly donated goods (that is over a half of its turnover comes from the sale of donated goods) is able to obtain rate relief. This will entitle it as of right to the 50 per cent mandatory rate relief, and it may also be able to obtain a further 50 per cent relief at the discretion of the local authority. It should be noted that this concession applies to any charity shop whatever the nature of the charity it benefits, whereas the eligibility for zero-rating for VAT purposes is confined to specific classes of charity only (*see previous section*).

The circumstances in which rate relief can be granted is dealt with much more fully in the section on Rates (*see section on Rates*).

The profits from charity shops

The money raised from the sale of donated goods by a charity is regarded by the Inland Revenue as a donation rather than a profit from trade. And as a donation, no tax is payable on the amount raised. A letter from the Inland Revenue to the Charity Trading Advisory Group dated 19th March 1981 makes this point clear: 'The proceeds of sale of out-and-out gifts would not normally be regarded as the trading profits of a charity. A person who gives a saleable article to a charity shop (in preference to selling it, for example) may be assumed to be making a voluntary contribution to the charity. In such circumstances the proceeds of sale are regarded as being the donation. Where therefore the goods sold by the charity consist solely of donated articles, it would not be necessary to set up a trading subsidiary in order to escape taxation. It would be a different matter of course if the items sold were of mixed origin.'

It is for this reason that charity shops selling donated goods are able to operate within the charity itself rather than through a separate trading company without becoming liable to pay tax on the 'profits' from their shops or falling foul of their charitable status by undertaking non-charitable trading activities. Oxfam, which runs the largest chain of charity shops in the country, organises its shops activity directly through its main charity, whereas its Christmas brochure and other trading activities are operated via a separate trading company established for the purpose called 'Oxfam Activities'. And the situation would be similar for the smallest charity which operated just one gift shop.

There are also concessions in respect of:

(a) Small-scale trading, such as jumble sales;

(b) Trading carried out directly by the charity within its primary purposes;

(c) Trading where the work in connection with the trade is carried out mainly by the beneficiaries of the charity, for example by the handicapped or disadvantaged people that the charity has been established to assist.

In all these instances the profit from trading will not be taxable. The whole subject of what trading is permitted by a charity and when tax is liable on the profits of the trade is dealt with more fully in the section on Charity Trading.

A charity shop which sells donated goods or goods produced by the charity as a primary purpose (eg. aids for the handicapped or publications) or goods produced by the beneficiaries of the charity or a mixture of goods in all three categories will not be liable to pay any tax on its profits. Where the charity shop is also selling commercial items it will be taxed on the profits arising from the sale of these commercial items, although any profits arising from the sale of donated items, etc. will not be taxable. If the trading activity is set up within a separate trading company which covenants back its profits to the main charity, then all tax liability will be avoided. It should be noted that tax is paid on the profits arising from the trade, and not on the turnover. If the sales of commercial items are at a modest level, after paying the cost price of the items and other incidental selling costs, the organisation might indeed be making very little or no profit on the sale of these items, and its liability to tax in consequence would be modest.

11. Value Added Tax

VAT is a wide-ranging tax on most supplies of goods or services in the domestic economy. The law on VAT is the *1972 Finance Act* (as amended by subsequent legislation) and the Orders and Regulations made under the Act. VAT is chargeable only where taxable supplies are made in the course or furtherance of any business by a person registrable for the tax. 'Business' in this context means the supply of goods or services made for a consideration. The motives of the 'business' and whether it is trading at a profit are both irrelevant. Some supplies are exempted from VAT, and some supplies are zero-rated (which means that they are taxable, but the rate of tax that is levied is zero).

To be eligible for VAT, there has to be a supply of goods or services for a consideration. Whether or not the consideration is commensurate with the supply is not normally a relevant factor in deciding whether VAT is chargeable. However, the supply by a charity of goods or services to distressed persons consistently below cost for the relief of their distress (*see below for further details*), the supply of any purely voluntary services given free of charge by charities in accordance with their objects, any donations received by charities freely given and not in return for any supply, and the religious activities of churches and other charities are all regarded as being non-business activities and therefore **outside the scope of the tax**.

There is a lot of confusion about the position of charities with regard to VAT. The general situation is that there is no general relief from VAT for charities purely because of their charitable status. A charity is in an identical position to any company, society, association, or individual regarding the tax, apart from a number of quite small concessions and the fact that some of their activities might be outside the scope of the tax.

The basic position is that:

(a) The charity is deemed to be a 'taxable person' for VAT. If a charity has branches which enjoy only limited autonomy in managing their business and financial affairs, that charity and its branches constitute a single entity for VAT registration purposes. On the other hand, local societies that are independent, separate bodies in their own right, having complete control of all their business and financial affairs, are separate entities for VAT registration purposes.

(b) If the sales of taxable goods and services made by the charity (including full-rated and zero-rated supplies) exceeds £17,000 in any year, the charity will be obliged to register for VAT. It will also be obliged to register if its taxable turnover exceeds £6,000 in any quarter, unless it can persuade Customs and Excise that its turnover for that quarter and the following three quarters will not exceed £17,000. These exemption limits are raised from time to time to take account of inflation, and the figures given here relate to 1982–83. If its taxable turnover is below the £17,000 limit, the charity may seek voluntary registration for VAT. Customs and Excise do not automatically accept applications for voluntary registration, but tend to give sympathetic consideration to applications from charities. In certain circumstances it may be advantageous for an organisation not obliged to register to seek voluntary registration (*see below*).

(c) A charity registered for VAT will charge its customers VAT at 15 per cent on all standard-rated supplies it makes and at 0 per cent on all zero-rated supplies. The sales of taxable supplies are known as 'outputs', and the tax charged by a supplier is known as 'output tax'.

(d) In respect of these outputs (the full-rated and zero-rated supplies it has made) it will calculate any VAT it has been charged on any goods or services it has purchased in the course of making these supplies. These goods and services are known as 'inputs', and the tax paid in making these purchases is known as 'input tax'.

(e) The charity will deduct the total of its input tax from the total of its output tax in any VAT accounting period and pay the balance to Customs and Excise. Where the total input tax exceeds the total output tax the charity will receive a payment from Customs and Excise.

Where the charity purchases goods or services which relate to its non-business activities the VAT paid by the charity on these purchases is not input tax and may not be recovered under any circumstances. Where the charity purchases goods or services which relate to its exempt supplies any VAT paid by the charity will not be deductible. Where particular purchases made by the charity relate to both taxable supplies and exempt supplies or non-business activities, an apportionment is made between the various activities in calculating the amount of input tax that is deductible. This is a complicated area beyond the scope of this publication.

The basic situation can be illustrated as follows:

Tax status of supply	VAT chargeable on supplies made by the charity	VAT paid on purchases made by the charity that relate to the supply
(a) For charities registered for VAT		
Non-business/ outside the scope	no VAT chargeable	not deductible
Exempt	no VAT chargeable	not deductible
Zero-rated	no VAT chargeable	deductible
Standard-rated	chargeable at full rate	deductible
(b) For charities not registered for VAT		
Any	no VAT chargeable	not deductible

Where a charity is operating below but near the registration limit for VAT, it should keep a close watch on the level of taxable supplies it is making. If, for example, the acceptance of sponsorship would bring it over the regulation limit, it may want to look for donations instead; or it may wish to consider devolving its jumble sales to autonomous local groups or its sales of Christmas cards to a separate trading company.

Where a charity is supplying zero-rated goods (or in certain instances where it is making full-rated supplies at below cost), it may find that its input tax exceeds its output tax, and that as a result it is a net beneficiary from VAT. It is seldom worth seeking voluntary registration on this count if the taxable turnover of the organisation is below the exemption limit, as the administrative hassle will not be worth the saving. In any case, Customs and Excise are reluctant to allow voluntary registration simply on the basis that they would then have to pay money to the organisation, although they do tend to give sympathetic consideration to applications from charities.

There are two attitudes that charities have towards VAT. The first is that it is a reasonable tax, well established in society, and that charities should live with it, pay it with good grace and budget for it in their fund-raising. The other attitude is that it is grossly unfair that organisations providing a charitable service should be required to pay the tax. Many activities undertaken by charities are deemed to be non-business activities and the VAT on purchases relating to these is not recoverable. Barnardo's reckon that they are paying £500,000 per annum in unrecoverable tax, the National Children's Home £280,000 and the Spastics Society £218,000. There are two pressures for relief to be given from VAT to charities:

(a) Arts organisations have consistently lobbied to get the sale of tickets for performances (such as theatres and concerts) zero-rated;

(b) A group of eight of the larger social welfare charities through the 'VAT Reform Group' have been lobbying to obtain VAT relief in respect of purchases made in the course of providing charitable services.

At the moment there is little indication that there will be any change in the foreseeable future. The main VAT provisions that affect charities are shown in the following sections.

Non-business activities of charities

The major impact of VAT as it affects charities is that much of what
they do is considered to be non-business activity. The charity will
not have to charge VAT on any non-business supplies it makes; but
at the same time it will be unable to recover any VAT paid on any
purchases made in the course of undertaking these non-business
activities. The main areas of non-business income and activity that
relate to charities are:

(a) Grants and donations

Donations, bequests or other voluntary contributions from the
public (such as the proceeds of flag days, house-to-house collections, etc.) received by charities are not deemed to be the proceeds of
business activity and are outside the scope of VAT. Any apportionment of input tax must take account of such non-business income.

Where a charity receives a grant which is to be used either to
provide a specific benefit to a particular person or for a specific
purpose of benefit to the person making the grant, the grant is
regarded as being a payment for a supply and is liable to tax.

(b) Voluntary services performed by charities

Any purely voluntary services given free of charge by charities in
accordance with their objects are deemed to be non-business
activities.

(c) Supplies made by charities consistently below cost

Where a charity supplies goods or services to distressed persons consistently below cost for the relief of their distress, such supplies are
regarded as non-business and outside the scope of the tax.

'Consistently below cost' means that the charges are always below
the actual monetary cost to the charity making the supply. In determining actual cost only out-of-pocket expenses should be taken into
account. Capital expenditure on buildings, notional charges for the
depreciation of capital assets, the creation of financial reserves
for repairs and maintenance (as opposed to any actual repair or

maintenance costs incurred during the year in question) and the notional cost of any unpaid labour provided by voluntary helpers should all be ignored in making the calculation.

The 'relief of distress' means either the relief of poverty or the making of provision for the cure or mitigation or prevention of, or for the care of persons suffering from or subject to, any disease or infirmity or disability affecting human beings (including the care of women before, during and after childbirth). Supplies (including the provision of subsidised holidays) by charities to elderly persons (eg. aged 65 years or more), to physically or mentally handicapped persons, to the chronically sick and to the poor are all regarded as being for the relief of distress.

When a charity registered for VAT supplies aids to handicapped persons, which are eligible for zero-rating, such supplies are treated as business supplies regardless of whether any or what charge is made, and the input tax may be deducted subject to the normal rules.

(d) Religious activities

The religious activities of churches and other charities are not regarded as business activities for VAT purposes. Fees or donations received by the clergy in connection with religious rites and offertories collected from congregations at religious services are therefore regarded as the proceeds of non-business activities outside the scope of VAT. If a church, parsonage board or similar body is registered for VAT in respect of a business activity and uses a building for both business and non-business activities, it may be able to recover a proportion of the tax on any repairs, maintenance, etc. of that building.

Concessions available to charities

1. Income treated as donated income and outside the scope of VAT

(a) Sale of tickets at special events

Admission to entertainments and other functions held in aid of charities is, in principle, liable to VAT. If a minimum charge is stipulated and any additional amount paid by the purchaser is completely and genuinely **an optional donation**, tax will be chargeable only on the stipulated minimum. The basic minimum charge must not be lower than the normal commercial charge. The fact that part of the charge is an optional donation must be made absolutely clear and advice on the wording used should be sought from Customs and Excise.

For a ticket selling at £20, a charity would receive £17.40 after paying VAT. For a ticket selling at £5 plus £15 optional donation, the charity would receive £19.35. In this example, if 13 per cent or more of those attending only paid the minimum charge then the charity would lose out. So care has to be taken to encourage the supporter to pay the higher price in full.

(b) Advertising in charity brochures

Advertisements in charity brochures are treated as donations if four conditions are met:

(a) The brochure is published by a charity and has the characteristics of a fund-raising exercise;

(b) Payments made by the advertiser are clearly excessive;

(c) The motivation of the advertiser is to support the charity;

(d) The brochure includes a significant proportion of private advertising.

In other circumstances the advertisement will be zero-rated if it appears in a periodical publication published more frequently than once a year, or standard-rated otherwise. (*See also the Section on Company Giving.*)

(c) Membership subscriptions

A membership subscription to a charity will be treated as a donation if no benefit is received by the member other than an annual report and voting rights. Where the member does receive some benefit the subscription will be liable to VAT. The amount of VAT charged will depend on the nature of the benefits provided to the member in return for his subscription. If the benefits are a mixture of standard-rated and zero-rated and exempt supplies, then an apportionment

will be made, and VAT will only be charged on a part of the subscription. Subscriptions to certain organisations including youth
clubs, professional bodies and trade unions are exempt from VAT.
(*See the section on Membership Subscriptions.*)

(d) Sponsorship

In certain circumstances a sponsorship payment may be considered
a donation, if the sponsor does not receive any supply of goods or
services as a result of the donation. Customs and Excise accept an
acknowledgement of the donation and even some measure of
publicity for this as reasonable. In general most sponsorship is considered a taxable supply. (*See the section on Company Giving.*)

2. Reliefs by way of zero-rating

Various purchases made by charities in connection with their
charitable work are zero-rated:

(a) Catering for meals-on-wheels

The supply to any charity or other voluntary body of prepared food
for onward supply for example through a meals-on-wheels service is
zero-rated.

(b) Taking books for the blind and handicapped

The supply to the Royal National Institute for the Blind, the
National Listening Library and other similar charities of machines,
related tapes, parts and certain office equipment designed or
specially adapted for use exclusively by the blind and severely handicapped are zero-rated.

(c) Wireless sets for the blind

The supply to a charity of wireless receiving sets solely for free loan
to the blind is zero-rated.

(d) Lifeboats

The supply to, and repair and maintenance for, the Royal National Lifeboats Institution (RNLI) of any lifeboats is zero-rated. This relief is specific to the RNLI and not available to any other organisation.

(e) Sale of donated goods

The sale of donated goods by a charity established primarily for the relief of distress or for the protection or benefit of animals, and the donation of such goods to a charity for the purpose of sale are zero-rated (*For full details of this concession see the section on Charity Shops.*)

(f) Aids for handicapped persons

The supply to a handicapped person for domestic or personal use or to a charity for the benefit of handicapped persons (whether by sale or donation) of certain equipment is zero-rated. In addition the supply of services for adapting or repairing such equipment is zero-rated. The eligible equipment includes: medical and surgical appliances designed solely for the relief of a severe abnormality or severe injury; adjustable beds for invalids; commode chairs, etc.; chair lifts, hoists and lifters; personal ambulances, being motor vehicles adapted to be suitable for carrying one passenger on a wheelchair or stretcher. Full details are given in *Group 14* of the *Zero Rate Schedule* and the explanatory leaflet *'Aids for Handicapped Persons'* which is available from Customs and Excise.

(g) Donated medical and scientific equipment, etc.

Certain medical and scientific equipment (and parts or accessories relating to such equipment) is zero-rated if it is purchased with funds provided by a charity or from voluntary contributions for use by a charitable institution providing care or medical or surgical treatment for chronically sick or disabled persons; or for donation to a non-profit hospital or research institution; or for donation to health authorities of the National Health Service. For goods that are donated, if the recipient of the goods is not a charity, it may not contribute any part of the purchase price.

The items eligible for this relief are: medical and scientific equipment solely for use in medical research, diagnosis or treatment; and ambulances. The relief relates to equipment only and does not include any consumable goods used in connection with it. The purchaser is required to notify the manufacturer or supplier that the purchase is eligible for this relief. Full details are given in *Group 16* of the *Zero Rate Schedule* and in the leaflet *'Donated Medical and Scientific Equipment, etc.'* which is available from Customs and Excise.

(h) Self-build construction

Normally the supply of any new building is zero-rated. But if an individual or a group constructs the building using their own labour they would not be eligible for relief on the input tax paid on the materials used in the construction and on other building services. There are special arrangements for an individual building for himself, and Customs and Excise have a scheme to enable non-profit groups to obtain the benefit of zero-rating on their purchases in relation to self-build projects. The scheme is outlined in the leaflet *'Charities and other bodies engaged in new building projects on a self-build or self-help basis'*, which is available from Customs and Excise.

3. Relief on Imports and Exports

The export of any goods by a charity is zero-rated. This allows any VAT on the purchases of goods by a charity for export to be reclaimed. This relief is only available to charities that are registered for VAT. If a small charity intends to send goods or equipment overseas it would be sensible for it to pay over the funds collected for the purpose to a charity that is registered for VAT which would purchase the goods and reclaim the VAT.

There are certain reliefs on imports made by charities:

(a) VAT (and any import duty that may be payable) may be waived on imported articles donated or loaned to non-profit organisations for their retention and use. Organisations eligible for this concession include charities, churches, schools, universities, social service organisations. This concession does not apply to tobacco or alcohol items or to goods donated for resale (which may be eligible for zero-rating relief). Requests for consideration under this concession should be made in advance of importation giving full particulars of the function of the organisation and the circumstances in which the gift is to be received. Requests should be addressed to VAT Administration Directorate, HM Customs and Excise, RDA Branch 2, Kings Beam House, Mark Lane, London EC3R 7HE.

(b) VAT (and any import duty that may be payable) may be waived on donated Christmas trees received by a town or a non-profit organisation from overseas for public display at Christmas time in connection with charitable activities, provided that the gift or its display has no advertising aspect. A licence issued by the appropriate Department of Agriculture will be necessary. Applications for this concession should be sent to the same address as (a) above.

(c) VAT relief is given on gifts of used clothing and medical supplies that are imported for re-export for disaster or emergency relief. Enquiries regarding transhipment procedures should be addressed to General Customs Directorate, HM Customs and Excise, Branch 3, Room 20/10, Kent House, Upper Ground, London SE1 9PS.

4. Exemptions from VAT

Certain services provided by charities and other organisations are exempted from VAT which means that the charity does not charge the consumer any VAT but also cannot reclaim VAT in respect of any purchases made in connection with these supplies.

(a) Subsidised Professional training

The provision otherwise than for profit of training or retraining for any trade profession or employment is an exempt supply. The organisation providing the training has to be able to demonstrate that it is being provided below cost and is being financed in whole or in part by other activities or from grants. Up until 1980 it was sufficient that the organisation had charitable status, but this is no longer the case and the exemption will not be so widely available. The supply of incidental items by the organisation to its own trainees is also exempt (course materials, catering, etc.).

Catering supplied by a caterer acting as agent to an organiser of exempt courses is also exempt. However, the definition of what is an agent is complex, and Customs and Excise are prepared to zero-rate any supplies of catering in connection with exempt training as being a supply to a catering establishment. The supply is thus treated as being of food and is zero-rated under *Group 1* of the *Zero Rate Schedule*.

(b) Education

Education by a school or university is exempt. When provided by another body, to be exempt it must be of a kind provided by a school or university and provided below cost. The supply of incidental materials by the organisation to its own students is also exempt. The supply of educational materials generally is not exempt, although the supply of books is zero-rated.

(c) Youth club facilities

Certain supplies by a youth club to its members in the normal course of its activities as a youth club are exempt. Supplies include facilities received in return for the membership together with any additional payments relating directly to cultural or recreational activities. It does not include charges for other entertainment or for food and drink. A youth club is regarded as being a non-profit organisation whose rules restrict membership to people under 20 years of age and which provides cultural and recreational activities for such persons. Where membership is not so restricted and is open to (young) people over 20 years of age, this exemption does not apply. (Subscriptions passed by the youth club on behalf of its members to regional or national HQ are not considered a taxable supply and are outside the scope of VAT; affiliation fees of the youth club to itself to its own regional or national association are covered by the exemption and are not taxable, but any other affiliation fees would be taxable.)

(d) Certain caring services

The provision of care or medical treatment to residents, infants or patients in certain types of institution is exempt. This includes registered nursing homes, registered residential homes for the mentally ill, registered homes for the elderly, for the disabled and for children, community homes, probation hostels, and registered day nurseries and playgroups. This has a wide application to charities. It also prevents them from recovering VAT on any taxable purchases made in connection with providing such supplies.

(e) Subscriptions to trade unions and professional bodies

This exemption is discussed in the section on 'Membership Subscriptions'.

(f) Entry fees for sports competitions

This exemption is discussed in the section on 'Betting, gaming and competitions'.

(g) Lotteries and gaming

The granting of a right to take part in a lottery (that is lottery income) is exempt. Betting and gaming income is exempt, but this does not include the admission to premises or the supply of a gaming machine.

5. VAT and printed matter

There is no difference between a charity and any other organisation with regard to the liability of printed matter to VAT. VAT is chargeable according to what is produced, and not how it is used nor how it is printed. But since print and publications are something that many charities are involved with, it is worth looking at some of the ways that charities can avoid paying VAT.

The general rule is that books, periodicals, newspapers, pamphlets and leaflets are zero-rated, whereas other matter is standard rated. Full details are given in the leaflet *'The liability to VAT of printed and similar matter'* available from Customs and Excise. Some common items that are not zero-rated are:

posters

handbills designed for display

folders of information

diaries and calendars

stationery (but not printed form letters, which are zero-rated)

postcards and greetings cards

material designed to be filled in such as record books, notebooks, exercise books

all services relating to the printed item supplied and invoiced separately

postage and packing.

There are several ways of avoiding VAT:

(a) Design

In certain circumstances it is possible to design a piece of printed matter so that it is not liable to VAT:

(i) A leaflet to be zero-rated should normally fall within the following guidelines: it should consist of a single sheet of paper not greater than A4 size and primarily designed to be held in the hand for reading by individuals rather than hung up for general display. It should be complete in itself and not part of a larger publication. It should contain a significant proportion of textual matter as opposed to illustrative matter. It should be supplied in sufficient quantity (at least 50) for general distribution. (It may be printed, instant printed, Xeroxed or duplicated.)

(ii) A leaflet or brochure where more than one quarter of the total publication is to be filled in and returned is standard-rated. This refers not to the area of the order form but to the size of the piece to be returned in relation to the whole (the fact that the reverse side of the order form may contain textual matter is not significant).

(iii) A loose-bound publication such as a Jackdaw information kit is standard-rated except where all the material consists of genuinely separate leaflets, pamphlets, booklets, where the item would be zero-rated.

VALUE ADDED TAX

(b) Dealing with the printer

Where an organisation is being charged VAT on an item which should be zero-rated, it is up to the organisation to point this out and get the VAT charge removed. The printer may not be aware of the VAT situation, and may simply charge VAT as a matter of course.

(c) Design services

Where an unregistered organisation is purchasing paper, design, typesetting, photographic and repro services that relate directly to a zero-rated publication, it would normally have to pay VAT on the purchase of these services (if the supplier is registered for VAT) and be unable to reclaim this. One possibility is for the purchaser to arrange to have the supplier invoice the printer, and then the printer will invoice the purchaser for the supply of a publication (which will include in the price charged all the services purchased in the course of producing the publication). The printer, who will be registered for VAT, will be able to reclaim the VAT that has been paid from Customs and Excise. The purchaser may be required to make stage payments to the printer in respect of the publication to cover the printer for any payments made by the printer to other suppliers. This is a relatively easy procedure to arrange, but it should be discussed at the same time as the printer is being chosen.

(d) Post and packing

Although VAT is not charged on postage stamps, the supply of postage and packing or of a postage or delivery charge to a customer is standard-rated. If the price of the article is quoted inclusive of post and packing and no separate charge is made for post and packing, then if the item is zero-rated, no VAT will be payable. Thus a book that sells for £1.95 post free is zero-rated, whereas VAT is charged on the postage charge if the price of the same book is quoted as £1.75 plus 20p postage. So an organisation might save money by having inclusive postage charges. But since the public are on the whole prepared to pay a reasonable charge for postage and packing, the same publication might well be priced at £1.95 plus 20p postage without loss of sales. How an organisation treats its post and packing will depend on individual circumstances. There is no single best method.

6. Further information

This section has described very briefly the VAT situation of charities and the concessions and reliefs that are available. For further information the reader should contact their local VAT office or read the relevant publications and leaflets available from Customs and Excise. The two main leaflets are the *General Guide (Notice 700)* and *Scope and Coverage (Notice 701)*.

For a complete list of VAT publications, contact:

HM Customs and Excise, VAT Administration Directorate, Kings Beam House, Mark Lane, London EC3.

The National Council for Voluntary Organisations run a VAT advisory service for charities. Queries on matters regarding VAT should be put to them in writing. They also publish two guides to VAT, a primary guide which can be obtained by any charity, and a secondary guide which is only available to charities registered for VAT. For further information, contact:

VAT Advisory Service, National Council for Voluntary Organisations, 26 Bedford Square, London WC1.

Registration of Charities

The trustees of a charity in England and Wales are obliged under the *1960 Charities Act* to seek registration with the Charity Commission, unless the charity falls into one of the excepted categories. During the registration process the Charity Commission will have to decide whether the applicant body has been or will be established for good charitable purposes. It will also seek the views of the Inland Revenue. Once the charity has been registered, the charity registration number provides conclusive proof of its charitable status; and provided the charity can show that it is applying its funds to charitable purposes, it will be able to obtain the benefits of charitable status.

Where a charity is required to register with the Charity Commission, the Charity Commission is the sole arbiter of charitable status. There are two other interested parties who may question any decision – the charity itself and the Inland Revenue. In the vast majority of cases there is agreement between all three parties. But if the charity feels that registration is being unfairly withheld, or if the Inland Revenue feels that the organisation is not (in their view) established for charitable purposes only, and therefore ought not to be a charity, then there is the right to appeal against the decision of the Charity Commission. Appeals can be made first to the Board of the Charity Commission and then to the High Court, the Court of Appeal and ultimately the House of Lords.

Although under *Section 4(2)* of the *1960 Charities Act* there is an obligation for a charity to register with the Charity Commission, there is no penalty for non-registration. If a charity which is not registered is claiming exemption from tax from the Inland Revenue, and if in fact the charity should be registered with the Charity Commission, the Inland Revenue will inform the trustees of their obligation to register and will not grant any exemption from tax until the Charity Commission has considered the application.

For charities that are not obliged to register, their charitable status will be determined by the Inland Revenue and the local Rating Authority when the charity is making a claim for tax exemption or for rates relief. Where a charity has had its charitable status determined by the Inland Revenue when making a claim for tax exemption, the local Authority will take this as evidence of its charitable status when determining its eligibility for rate relief. The VAT concessions available from Customs and Excise on the whole are not available to all charities simply as a consequence of their charitable status, but are available to particular classes of charity only; and Customs and Excise will assess a charity's eligibility for VAT relief according to the criteria it uses for the particular relief the charity is seeking.

The following charities are not obliged to register:

(a) All charities in Scotland and Nothern Ireland

The jurisdiction of the Charity Commission does not extend to these parts of the United Kingdom and no register of charities is maintained for charities operating in Scotland and Northern Ireland at the present time; although there are proposals that registers should be established for charities operating in these parts of the United Kingdom.

(b) Exempt charities

These are mainly large institutions for which Parliament has provided other supervision (including universities, colleges, Eton, Winchester, the British Museum, the Church Commissioners, etc.). They also include any charity which is a registered Industrial and Provident Society within the meaning of the *1965 Industrial and Provident Societies Act* or a registered Friendly Society or branch within the meaning of the *1974 Friendly Societies Act*.

(c) Excepted charities

Certain charities have been excepted individually from registration by an order made by the Charity Commissioners. Some classes of charity have been excepted by a Statutory Regulation made under the Charities Act; these include:

(i) voluntary schools with no permanent endowment other than premises (*S.I. 1960 No: 2366*);

(ii) funds not representing permanent endowments being accumulated for the purpose of local units of the Boy Scouts Association or the Girl Guides Association (*S.I. 1961 No: 21044*);

(iii) charities mainly or wholly concerned with the advancement of religion (*S.I. 1963 No: 2074, S.I. 1964 No: 1825*). For further details see Leaflet RE4R on the '*Registration of Religious Charities*' available from the Charity Commission. The main categories of religious charities not required to register are:

> Charities for the religious purposes of the Church of England, the Methodists, the Baptists, the Congregationalists, the Independent Evangelical Churches, the Presbyterian Churches of England and Wales, the Society of Friends, the Unitarians. For these charities there are registration procedures with the official denominational body, and registration with this body relieves the charity of the obligation to register itself with the Charity Commission.

> Certain small funds which do not produce an income of more than £100 per annum for the general purposes of any bodies or groups of persons who exist to make provision for public religious worship.

> Certain small funds for the advancement of religion producing an income of not more than £50 per annum for the purposes of keeping a grave, tomb or personal monument in good order.

(iv) Charities concerned with the promotion of the efficiency of the armed forces with no interest in land other than a yearly tenancy, exclusively for the benefit of people serving in the armed forces, and not being a charity for the exhibition or preservation of articles of historical interest. (*S.I. 1965 No: 1056*).

(d) Small charities

Small charities which have neither (i) any permanent endowment (that is property held as capital and subject to a restriction on its being expended as income); nor (ii) income from investments and other property exceeding £15 per annum; nor (iii) the use and occupation of any land (including buildings). To be excepted as a small charity, a charity must satisfy all three of these conditions.

(e) Places of religious worship

Places of religious worship registered under the *1855 Places of Worship Registration Act*. This exception also extends to a vestry or caretaker's house situated on the same site as the place of worship and held on the same trusts, but it does not extend to any other buildings adjacent to the place of worship.

(f) Charitable appeals

Charitable appeals to the public by way of flag days, bazaars, entertainments or similar efforts which are organised for the benefit of specific charities. Those appeals where they are organised independently of the charity are not therefore considered to be charities and do not have to register as charities. They are subject to the restrictions for house-to-house or street collections and are regulated by the local Licensing Authority (the Metropolitan Police in London and the District Council elsewhere).

Even though a charity is excepted from the requirements to register, its trustees may still apply for the charity to be registered voluntarily, and the Charity Commission may, if it sees fit, register it. Such a charity may be removed from the register either on the decision of the Charity Commission or at the request of the charity (and on such a request the Charity Commission shall be obliged to remove the charity from the register).

With any application for a charity to be registered, the charity is required to supply a copy of its trust deed together with any other documents or information as may be requested by the Charity Commissioners. Once registered, the charity may if it wishes submit its Annual Accounts to the Charity Commission; it is only obliged to do this if it has a permanent endowment, or if the Charity Commission requests it to do so (for certain charities there are specific regulations relieving the charity of the obligation to submit its Annual Accounts).

As at the end of 1981, there were 139,289 charities on the Register of Charities. During that year 3,495 charities were registered and 254 charities were removed from the Register, mostly because they had been wound up or had ceased to operate. Of the 3,495 charities registered, 1,822 were new charities founded during the year and the remainder were charities which had not been obliged to register previously.

The Register of Charities is open to public inspection. The registered particulars of charities operating South of a line drawn roughly from the Bristol Channel to the Wash and of charities operating over the whole or a substantial part of England and Wales are normally kept at the offices of the Charity Commission in London (*57–60 Haymarket, London SW1Y 4QX*). Details of charities operating North of this line in England (but not Scotland) or in Wales are kept at the offices of the Charity Commission in Liverpool (*Graeme House, Derby Square, Liverpool L2 7SB*). Copies of this information for any particular charity will be supplied on request to any person on payment of the cost of transcription. There are three indexes of all charities on the Central Register kept at both offices. These indexes are classified by the name of the charity; by the purpose for which the charity is established; and by the area of operation of the charity. Local councils have the power (but not the duty) to keep an index of local charities operating in their area and this is undertaken by some authorities; and where such a local index is kept, it is open to inspection.

The charitable status of an organisation should not be confused with the legal status under which it is constituted. A charity can be a trust or a company limited by guarantee or a Friendly Society or an Industrial and Provident Society or even an unincorporated association established for a charitable purpose with a simple constitution drawn up by the committee. A charitable company limited by guarantee is required to register under the *Companies Act* and submit the required information to the Registrar of Companies, including its founding documents and its audited Annual Accounts. This is in addition to any requirements under the *Charities Act* with regard to information that has to be supplied to the Charity Commission. A society registered as a Friendly Society or as an Industrial and Provident Society is relieved of registration with the Charity Commission, but must fulfil the obligations imposed on it by the Registrar of Friendly Societies (*17 North Audley Street, London W1*). A charitable trust or any other unincorporated charity has no other requirements regarding registration or the supply of information beyond what is required by the Charity Commission, except that the Inland Revenue may well ask for detailed information before granting the charity tax relief in any particular tax year (and such information would have to be supplied by any charity, however it were constituted, if the tax relief were to be obtained).

If an organisation is established for charitable purposes only it will continue to be a charity so long as it exists. There is some confusion as to what happens if the charity goes beyond its charitable objects and applies its funds to purposes which are not charitable. There are two completely separate aspects of what might happen; the first relates to the Inland Revenue and the second to the Charity Commission.

The Inland Revenue, if it feels that the funds of the Charity are not being applied to charitable purposes, can take taxation action. It can refuse to grant exemption and not pay claims for repayment of tax to the charity. This can happen either when the Inland Revenue believes that the charity is accumulating funds to no purpose or when it believes that the funds are being misapplied. The Inland Revenue have an accounts examination section to keep a watch on what charities are doing. It is actually very difficult to keep an effective watch on all of the 139,289 registered charities and the large number of unregistered charities on top of this. The monitoring of charities is hampered both by lack of resources and by the difficulty in getting any real information from charities. In practice most bona fide charities will seldom encounter problems with the Inland Revenue. Any action that the Inland Revenue does take is confidential, and the Inland Revenue is not empowered to divulge any information on the activities of particular charities to the Charity Commission.

If the Charity Commission feels that the charity is not operating charitably, then it has a number of actions open:

(a) The first stage is normally to discuss the problem with the Trustees who might be able to give a satisfactory explanation of what they have been doing. Failing this, the Charity Commission will probably wish to seek an undertaking from the Trustees as to their future actions.

(b) If the Trustees refuse to give such an undertaking or continue to apply funds to purposes which are not charitable, then the

Inland Revenue would seek to remove the Trustees and to replace them with Trustees who were prepared to operate within the objects of the charity.

(c) The Trustees are responsible for the charity money and if they are misapplying the funds of the charity, action can be taken against them through the Courts to reclaim any funds that have been misapplied. It is extremely rare that the situation reaches this stage, but it is a threat which can persuade Trustees that they have to operate within the charitable objects of the charity. The liability of the Trustees in such a situation is not affected by whether the charity is incorporated as a limited liability company or not.

(d) The Charity Commission might also seek to review the objects of the charity. If as a result of such a review the Charity Commission reaches a decision that the objects are not now held to be wholly charitable, they have the power to remove the organisation from the Register of Charities.

The deregistration of a charity is not a normal procedure, as it will normally be found that most charities are established for good charitable objects. Deregistration is only something that will be resorted to if it is impossible for the charity to act charitably. It is a general principal of charity law that the Trusts under which charitable money are held are paramount and the Trustees are the (temporary) stewards of the charitable funds responsible for seeing that the charity operates within its objects. If the Trustees of the charity are misapplying the charity's funds, then this does not mean that the charity is not a charity or will cease to be a charity.

Appendix 2

Political activity by charities

An organisation may only be registered as a charity if its objects are exclusively charitable. And if its objects are exclusively charitable, it will be obliged to register (in England and Wales) unless it falls into one of the excused or excluded categories. Once it has been registered as a charity it may only act in pursuit of its objects. So charities are constrained by two sets of factors: firstly by what is held to be charitable and what is not; and secondly by the powers conferred on the charity through its constitution and, in particular, through its objects clause.

This is the basic guideline for charitable activity. There are several areas where a charity might come unstuck:

(a) By undertaking work which, although charitable, is outside its own charitable objects. The problem here is that the trustees would be misapplying the funds of the charity, which they are only permitted to apply to the objects of the charity. It may be that the trust deed no longer gives the trustees sufficient powers to undertake the work they feel necessary in the light of what they perceive to be today's needs. In this case the charity might seek to have its trust deed altered, or the trustees might consider setting up a new charity with wider objects to undertake the sort of work they wish to do.

(b) By undertaking work which is not in fact charitable. What is charitable and what is not charitable is determined by charity law. Charity law in this sense means case law built up over the years by decisions of the High Court, by the process of analogy, the starting point being the preamble to an Act of Parliament of 1601. The concept of charity has thus been evolving over 350 years, and the modern scope of charitable endeavour (which includes such diverse objects as the protection of the environment, the rehabilitation of drug offenders

156

and aid for Third World countries) is far wider than the original limited compass. There is nevertheless a view that court decisions on what is held to be charitable do not keep the legal understanding of charity entirely in line with a rapidly changing social environment and that consequently much well-intentioned work falls outside the net and is not in fact charitable. For example, seeking to reduce unemployment is not a charitable purpose, although mitigating the effects of unemployment might well be covered by 'relief of poverty or distress' which is a good charitable object. Self-help projects are not normally charitable as they are not for 'public benefit'. If an organisation wishes to undertake non-charitable 'good work' this cannot properly be done with the benefit of charitable status, as a charity must be established for charitable purposes only. The solution here would be for the non-charitable work to be carried out by an organisation which is not a charity.

(c) By undertaking commercial activities. Many charities trade extensively sometimes quite legitimately, within their charitable objects, usually to raise money or get publicity or otherwise promote the organisation. But trading is not of itself a charitable purpose, and where a charity gets too involved in trading activities, it might find that this will jeopardise its charitable status. This is very much a question of balance. There are also important tax considerations regarding any profits arising from its trading that a charity will have to take into account. If a charity wishes to trade at a level beyond what is acceptable, this has to be done via a separate trading company. The issues here are discussed in the sections on 'Charity Trading' and 'Charity Shops'.

There is a fourth area which is of particular importance to those organisations which not only seek to provide some charitable service, but which also seek to remove the causes of poverty or injustice or whatever has caused the need for the work they are doing. This is the extent that charities are able to involve themselves in campaigning and political activity.

This is a 'grey area' which has been of continuing concern to many charities and to the Charity Commission alike. Some charities are completely unsure of what they are allowed to do, and they

157

therefore restrain themselves from undertaking activities which would in fact be quite permissible. Others do get involved in campaigns but are unclear of the guidelines they should adhere to or what the consequences are if they overstep the mark.

In its Annual Report for 1969 the Charity Commision first drew up a set of principles which described what was permissible and what was not permissible. This also identified the 'grey areas' in between, where the situation could not be clearly defined and where much depended on attitudes and balance. In the intervening years, further comments and refinements have been made; and in its Annual Report for 1981 a second set of guidelines were issued, which better reflected the current situation. These do not say anything that was not already known, but they combine the whole of the present thinking of the Charity Commission on the subject of political involvement by charities. These new guidelines are printed below. But first a number of points should be made:

(a) The term 'political involvement' generally refers to involvement in party political activity or the promotion of legislative change. The reasons why trusts which promote changes in the law are not accepted as charitable were neatly summarised by Mr Justice Slade in the Amnesty International case, *McGovern and others v. Attorney General and Another (Amnesty International Trust) 1982*: 'First, the Courts would ordinarily have no sufficient means of judging, as a matter of evidence, whether the proposed change will or will not be for the public benefit. Second, even if the evidence suffices it to form a prima facie opinion that a change in the law is desirable, it must still decide the case on the principle that the law is right as it stands, since to do otherwise would be to usurp the functions of the legislature.' So because a charity must always exist for public benefit, and because the Courts (which are the final arbiters of what constitute a charitable purpose) cannot usurp the sovereignty of Parliament by declaring that a proposed change in the law will or will not be for the public benefit, it follows that a charity cannot legitimately seek to change the law. This does not mean that charities cannot suggest areas for reform − many do. And in fact many go further than this without encountering problems with the Charity Commission. It is probably true that the more

POLITICAL ACTIVITY BY CHARITIES

controversial the subject, the more careful the charity has to be in advocating any changes to the law. For example, in the fields of abortion or race relations or animal welfare, strong passions can be aroused and there are always people prepared to bring matters to the attention of the Charity Commission if they feel a charity is overstepping the mark. It is quite permissible for a charity to lobby for the law to be implemented, and it is also permissible for a charity to lobby for more resources to be allocated on particular areas of government (or local government) expenditure, or for it (the charity) to be given a grant for its work. Neither of these actions challenges the legal status quo.

(b) In many circumstances the Charity Commission will have no current information on their files relating to the day-to-day activities of any particular charity unless the charity maintains a high profile nationally. Problems will normally occur when someone (usually someone hostile to the policies of the Trustees of the charity) refers the activities of the charity to the Charity Commission for consideration or if the charity itself approaches the Charity Commission for clarification.

(c) The most usual outcome of any complaint, if proved justified, is for the matter to be discussed between the Charity Commission and the charity. The Commission will probably only try to seek assurances for the future. This will normally be sufficient, and it is unlikely in practice that the trustees will be surcharged for misapplying the funds of the charity. Provided the charity is held to have good charitable objects, it will not be removed from the Register as the result of any political activity. But where there is evidence that the trustees are wilfully and persistently applying the funds of their charity for purposes outside the legitimate scope of charitable endeavour, the Commissioners may refer the matter to the Attorney General so that consideration can be given to instituting action against the trustees for breach of trust. Also, the Inland Revenue may seek to withdraw any exemption from tax in relation to any funds that have not been applied for charitable purposes.

(d) Although this is not an invitation to anyone to undertake any amount of campaigning work through a charity, it does put the situation into a more realistic context than simply stating the ground rules. If an organisation or the people working for it wish to campaign beyond the limits set by the Charity Commission, a number of possibilities exist:

(i) The individuals can undertake the campaigning work as individuals, clearly distancing themselves from the charity and not spending any funds that belong to the charity.

(ii) The organisation need not seek registration as a charity and can operate as a non-charitable non-profit organisation. Amnesty International, the National Anti-Vivisection Society and the National Council for Civil Liberties are all examples of non-charitable campaigning organisations. The first two have applied for charitable status and been refused. The NCCL has a parallel charitable trust, the Cobden Trust, which it established to undertake its charitable educational work and obtain the tax benefits available on any funds raised for this work.

(iii) The organisation can set up a separate campaigning organisation to undertake non-charitable work, using non-charitable funds or money donated specifically for the campaigning work. War on Want have done this by setting up WoW Campaigns Ltd to operate alongside the main charity and campaign against the causes of poverty.

So the mechanisms are there for any organisation to undertake any political or campaigning work as the promoters of the organisation wish. But the charity must understand the law and organise itelf accordingly. The general principle must be adhered to that charitable and political work must be kept separate if the tax advantages of charitable status are to be obtained; and no tax advantages are available for organisations that are not established **for charitable purposes only**.

The *1981 Report of the Charity Commissioners for England and Wales* summarised the current view of the Commission regarding political activity by charities. *Sections 51 and 53–56* of that Report are reprinted here with the permission of HMSO:

The extent to which it is permissible for charities to promote, support or take part in political activities is not an area in which it is possible to lay down hard and fast rules. Each case has to be considered individually in the light of all the relevant circumstances and trustees should not hesitate to consult their legal advisers or seek our advice. The law has to be derived from a small number of decided cases. It is possible to deduce certain basic principles, and it may be helpful initially to set these out (as they were, in our view, before the Amnesty case which has confirmed and amplified the position):

(i) *A trust for the attainment of a political object is not charitable since the Court has no way of judging whether a proposed change in the law will or will not be for the public benefit* – Bowman v. Secular Society Ltd. [*1917*].

(ii) *To promote changes in the law, or maintenance of the existing law, is a political purpose and not charitable* – re Hopkinson [*1949*].

(iii) *To seek, not necessarily particular legislation, but a particular line of political administration or policy, is a political purpose and is not charitable* – re Hopkinson [*1949*].

(iv) *Political propaganda in the guise of education is not charitable* – re Hopkinson [*1949*].

(v) *The word 'political' is not necessarily confined to party politics. Any purpose of influencing legislation is a political purpose and is not charitable* – Inland Revenue Commissioners v. Temperance Council of Christian Churches of England and Wales [*1926*].

(vi) *A trust for the education of the public in one particular set of political principles is not charitable (although education in political matters generally could be)* – Bonar Law Memorial Trust v. Inland Revenue Commissioners [*1933*].

(vii) *Although an association for promoting some change in the law cannot itself be a charity (see (i) and (ii) above), an association would not necessarily lose its right to be considered a*

161

charity if, as a matter of construction, the promotion of legislation were one among other lawful purposes ancillary to good charitable purposes: it is a question of degree – National Anti-Vivisection Society v. Inland Revenue Commissioners [1943–47].

(viii) Research, to be charitable, must be directed to increasing the store of communicable knowledge in a public, as opposed to a private, way – re Hopkins' Will Trusts [1965].

The implications for charity trustees of the present state of the law – as confirmed by the Amnesty case – may be summarised as:

(i) Trustees who stray too far into the field of political activity:

(a) risk being in breach of trust;

(b) risk being held personally liable to repay to the charity the funds spent on such activity; and

(c) risk losing some tax relief for their charity, since this may be claimed only in respect of income applied to charitable purposes.

(ii) Political activity by the trustees would not necessarily affect the charitable status of the institution or be a reason for removing it from the Central Register of Charities; but

(iii) If the trustees could validly claim that the expressed purposes of the institution were wide enough to cover political activities, doubt would arise whether those purposes were exclusively charitable and, if the institution was registered as a charity, upon the correctness of the registration.

The following guidelines may be of help for the general guidance of charity trustees:

(i) A charity should undertake only those activities which can reasonably be said to be directed to achieving its purposes and which are within the powers conferred by its governing instrument;

(ii) To avoid doubt being cast on the claim of an institution to be a charity, its governing instrument should not include

power to exert political pressure except in a way that is merely ancillary to a charitable purpose. Whether a particular provision in the governing instrument of an institution is a substantive object or an ancillary object or power is a matter of the construction of the instrument. In general, what is ancillary is that which furthers the work of the institution, not something that will procure the performance of similar work by, for example, the Government of the day.

(iii) *The powers and purposes of a charity should not include power to bring pressure to bear on the Government to adopt, alter, or maintain a particular line of action. It is permissible for a charity, in furtherance of its purposes, to help the Government to reach a decision on a particular issue by providing information and argument, but the emphasis must be on rational persuasion.*

(iv) *A charity can spend its funds on the promotion of public general legislation only if in doing so it is exercising a power which is ancillary to and in furtherance of its charitable purposes.*

(v) *If a charity's objects include the advancement of education, care should be taken not to overstep the boundary between education and propaganda in promoting that object: for example, the distribution of literature urging the Government to take a particular course, or urging sympathisers to apply pressure to Members of Parliament for that purpose, would not be education in the charitable sense.*

(vi) *A charity which includes the conduct of research as one of its objects must aim for objectivity and balance in the method of conducting research projects; and in publishing the results of the research must aim to inform and educate the public, rather than to influence political attitudes or inculcate a particular attitude of mind.*

(vii) *Charities, whether they operate in this country or overseas, must avoid:*

    (a) *Seeking to influence or remedy those causes of poverty which lie in the social, economic and political structures of countries and communities.*

(b) *Bringing pressure to bear on a government to procure a change in policies or administrative practices (for example, on land reform, the recognition of local trade unions, human rights, etc.).*

(c) *Seeking to eliminate social, economic, political or other injustice.*

Unless its governing instrument precludes it from doing so, a charity may, generally speaking, freely engage in activities of the following kinds:

(i) *Where the Government or a governmental agency is considering or proposing changes in the law and invites comments or suggestions from charities, they can quite properly respond.*

(ii) *Where a Green or White Paper is published by the Government, a charity may justifiably comment.*

(iii) *Where a Parliamentary Bill has been published, a charity is justified in supplying to Members of either House such relevant information and arguments to be used in debate as it believes will assist the furtherance of its purposes.*

(iv) *Where a Bill would give a charity wider powers to carry out its purposes, it can quite properly support the passage of the Bill; and it can support or oppose any Private Bill relevant to its purposes, since private legislation does not normally have a political character.*

(v) *Where a question arises as to whether a Government grant is to be made or continued to a particular charity, the charity is entitled to seek to persuade Members of Parliament to support its cause.*

(vi) *Where such action is in furtherance of its purposes, a charity may present to a Government Department a reasoned memorandum advocating changes in the law.*

In suggesting these guidelines to trustees, we are not purporting to say that certain activities are morally, socially, or politically wrong or undesirable or that they ought not to be done; but that it is not permissible for them to be carried out by a charity, according to our understanding of the law. We are concerned only with the law and must seek to ensure that funds and other property impressed with charitable trusts are used for the purposes of those trusts and not for purposes which the law does not accept as charitable. We are always willing to give further advice on any specific problem a charity may have in this connection; for example, on the distinction between education and propaganda, or between an ancillary purpose and a main purpose, and to consider the drafts of any publications such as advertisements, appeals, newsletters, etc, on which trustees have doubts.

These guidelines need to be put into the perspective of how the Charity Commission actually monitors charities, and what will happen to a charity if it oversteps the mark. One should also note that in formulating a set of guidelines, the Charity Commission has inevitably erred on the side of caution, and therefore the situation probably appears much more restrictive than it actually is. It is also true to say that a charity seeking registration will come under closer scrutiny than one already on the register. Francis Gladstone in his book on charity law reform '*Charity, Law and Social Justice*' concludes that 'on the whole established charities seem not to be greatly hampered by the Charity Commission's guidelines – for once you are in the Club, the rules are not very strenuously applied. Where the guidelines do seem to cause real problems is in relation to new applications for registration.'

And despite the guidelines 'grey areas' still exist, particularly in deciding what is pressure and what is persuasion, what is ancillary and what is central, and what is education and what is propaganda. In certain instances the guidelines are more restrictive than what has been decided as a result of the cases considered by the Courts. Although the Charity Commission is the arbiter of charitable status, it is subject to appeal to the Courts. So if a charity believes that the guidelines have been drawn up too restrictively, it can disregard them. But eventually it may have to argue its case in the Courts – although few charities have sufficient funds to pay the costs of doing this. It is possible that a charity may have a perspective on what is 'political' which does not correspond with that of the Charity Commission. For example, the guidelines state that a charity 'must avoid seeking to influence or remedy those causes of poverty which lie in the social, economic and political structures of countries and communities'. But what does this mean? And a charity might reasonably believe that poverty is well and truly rooted in the social, economic and political structure. What then? This is a rhetorical question, because what charities can do is broadly delineated by what charities do do. By looking at the general pattern of political activity that charities do undertake one will probably get a better perspective of what is permissible than by a close study of the guidelines.

Appendix 3

Resources

1. Useful publications

COVENANTS: a practical guide to the tax advantages of giving, £3.95
A very detailed handbook on covenants, which explains how they work and how to take full advantage of them.

CHARITY STATUS: a practical handbook, £3.95
A basic, easy to read guide to charitable status, what it is and how to get it.

CHARITIES, SOCIAL WELFARE AND THE LAW, £10
A comprehensive and important book on charity law set in the context of its historical evolution and related to contemporary needs (*published by Weidenfeld and Nicolson, 91 Clapham High Street, London SW4, and available from bookshops*).

CHARITY, LAW AND SOCIAL JUSTICE, £4.95
A new guide to charity law and the need for reform. It presents itself as a reasoned memorandum, discussing the frontiers of charity and suggesting two options: a new start and piecemeal reform (*available from the NCVO*).

LOTTERIES AND GAMING, £1.95
A guide to the law for charities (*available from the NCVO*).

CHARITABLE GIVING AND TAXATION, £7.50
A regularly updated guide to all aspects of charitable giving and taxation (*available from Craigmyle, The Grove, Harpenden, Herts.*)

167

CHARITABLE DEEDS OF COVENANT: their meaning, application and management, £4
A good guide to the details of administering covenants (*available from the Charities Aid Foundation*).

CHARITIES AND VOLUNTARY ORGANISATIONS: The Honorary Treasurer, £2.95
A guide to charities, taxation and the role of the treasurer (*available from the Institute of Chartered Accountants in England and Wales, Moorgate Place, London EC2*).

CHARITY TRADING HANDBOOK, £4.95
A comprehensive guide to all aspects of charity trading.

REPORTS OF THE CHARITY COMMISSIONS FOR ENGLAND AND WALES
An annual report of the work of the Charity Commission and of issues affecting charities (including legal cases, campaigning and political activities and other matters of interest). Published in June each year (*available from HMSO*).

VAT PUBLICATIONS FROM HM CUSTOMS AND EXCISE
HM Customs and Excise have a range of guides and explanatory leaflets on VAT which are referred to in the Section on VAT (*available from local VAT Offices of HM Customs and Excise*).

The following fund-raising handbooks from Directory of Social Change may also be of interest:

RAISING MONEY FROM TRUSTS, £2.95
RAISING MONEY FROM GOVERNMENT, £2.95
RAISING MONEY FROM INDUSTRY, £2.95
INDUSTRIAL SPONSORSHIP AND JOINT PROMOTIONS, £2.95

All the books mentioned here can be obtained from the Directory of Social Change, except where otherwise stated. Please add 40p per book to cover postage and packing. Orders should be addressed to Publications Dept., Directory of Social Change, 9 Mansfield Place, London NW3.

2. Useful organisations

INLAND REVENUE
Head Office, Somerset House, Strand, London WC2
Capital Taxes Office, Minford House, Rockley Road, London W14
Claims Branch (for England, Wales and Northern Ireland), Magdalen House, Trinity Road, Bootle, Merseyside
Claims Branch (for Scotland), Trinity Park House, South Trinity Road, Edinburgh EH5

HM CUSTOMS AND EXCISE
VAT Administration Directorate, Kings Beam House, Mark Lane, London EC3
Local branches (see Telephone Directory for addresses)

CHARITY COMMISSION
Head Office, 14 Ryder Street, London SW1
Register of Charities (for Southern England), 57–60 Haymarket, London SW1
Register of Charities (for Northern England and Wales), Graeme House, Derby Square, Liverpool L2

REGISTRAR OF FRIENDLY SOCIETIES
17 North Audley Street, London W1

CHARITIES AID FOUNDATION
48 Pembury Road, Tonbridge, Kent
CAF provides a range of services for donors to charity.

NATIONAL COUNCIL FOR VOLUNTARY ORGANISATIONS
26 Bedford Square, London WC1
NCVO has a library and information service which provides regular information on matters affecting charities.

CHARITY TRADING ADVISORY GROUP
9 Mansfield Place, London NW3
CTAG provides advice and help on all aspects of charity trading.

RESOURCES

ASSOCIATION FOR BUSINESS SPONSORSHIP OF THE ARTS
12 Abbey Churchyard, Bath
ABSA can provide advice on aspects of taxation and sponsorship and has two pamphlets on the subject.

170